To

....

From

....

Date

....

© 2022 by Barbour Publishing, Inc.

Print ISBN 978-1-63609-312-3

Cover Design: Greg Jackson, Thinkpen Design

Published by Barbour Publishing, Inc., 1810 Barbour Drive, Uhrichsville, Ohio 44683, www.barbourbooks.com.

Our mission is to inspire the world with the life-changing message of the Bible.

Printed in China.

PRAYERFUL
Living

Devotions
to Encourage
a Woman's
Heart

HILARY BERNSTEIN

BARBOUR
PUBLISHING

A Prayerful Life
Is a Beautiful Life

Prayer is an amazing gift. With just a thought, you can communicate with the Creator of the universe. The Lord is a God who sees, knows, and hears. And He hears each and every one of your prayers. *Prayerful Living* examines what God's Word reveals about prayer and relates the biblical truth to your life. As you read this book, my hope is not only that you'll learn about the Lord's plans and purpose for prayer but also that you'll feel compelled to pray to Him at absolutely any time for absolutely any reason. Please take the time to consider why you should pray, how you can pray, and what prayer has accomplished in the past. God is faithful, and He loves you very much. He wants to hear from you, and He wants you to get to know Him better and more intimately through the prayers you pray. Enjoy the strength and beauty of a prayerful life!

—Hilary Bernstein

Always Heard

I love the LORD, because he has heard my voice and
my pleas for mercy. Because he inclined his ear to me,
therefore I will call on him as long as I live.

PSALM 116:1–2 ESV

Have you ever needed to communicate something very important, but you couldn't reach the person who needed your message? Maybe you tried calling or texting someone with a time-sensitive question but had to wait a long time for a reply. Or maybe you faced an emergency and couldn't find the one person you really needed to tell.

While those times are nerve racking and frustrating, you never need to worry about experiencing such a moment with the Lord. The Lord hears your voice when you call out to Him. When you've had all you can handle and plead for mercy, He hears and knows. When you call on Him at any time of the day, He's listening. In fact, He never gets tired of hearing you. He wants to be a part of your life and always listens when you call out to Him.

Father, thank You for listening. What a relief to know
that no matter what, You'll always hear my prayers.
Your care and concern are so comforting. Thank You!

7

The Antidote to Overwhelm

After He had sent the crowds away, He went up on the mountain
by Himself to pray; and when it was evening, He was there alone.

MATTHEW 14:23 NASB

When you're in the middle of a hectic day or busy season of life, any extra request can feel overwhelming. Even the smallest question can feel like an unbearable added weight. It's easy to snap when you feel under pressure.

During His time on this earth, Jesus experienced requests and demands that would overwhelm anyone else. Crowds of people sought Him out for healing and miracles. Enemies tried to twist His words and plot against Him. His closest friends needed teaching and guidance. Yet Jesus gave and gave of Himself every day.

What was behind His endless compassion and willingness to meet the needs of others? Prayer. Getting away by Himself to spend time with His Father was key. No matter what His day looked like, He still went away to pray alone.

The next time you feel pulled in all directions, remember to get away by yourself and pray for a while. It will change and center you more than you can imagine!

Father, when I'm busy, stressed, and overwhelmed
by life's demands, please help me take the
time to get away and pray to You!

Are You Listening?

*"Call to me and I will answer you and tell you great
and unsearchable things you do not know."*

JEREMIAH 33:3 NIV

Far too often, it's easy to think of prayer as an opportunity to talk to God. Of course, you can cry out to Him at absolutely any time. And He does want you to come to Him with all your cares, concerns, and requests.

But do you stop to consider prayer as a time to listen for God and His response? The Lord promises to answer you when you call to Him. And what will He tell you? Great, unsearchable things you don't already know.

Just as a good conversation includes both talking and truly listening to hear what the other person is communicating, prayer includes both talking and listening too. You definitely should feel open to share absolutely anything and everything with your heavenly Father. But you also should be ready and willing to listen to Him. He just might surprise you with all He wants to communicate with you.

Father, I love pouring out my heart to You. I need to do a
better job of listening to You, though. Please help me wait
patiently for Your answer. I can hardly wait to hear the
great and unsearchable things You want to share with me!

Too Deep for Words

Likewise the Spirit helps us in our weakness. For we do not know what to pray for as we ought, but the Spirit himself intercedes for us with groanings too deep for words.

ROMANS 8:26 ESV

Sometimes there simply are no words for feelings. In fact, sometimes thoughts don't even make sense. Have you ever felt "off" but couldn't explain the exact reasons? Or have you ever felt completely broken-hearted but couldn't express your grief in words? Maybe you experienced a confusing mixture of sadness, disappointment, anger, and shock.

Because the Lord formed you and knows you, He knows that sometimes feelings are so much more intense than words can express. The Holy Spirit, who is fully God, comes to live in believers once they've accepted Christ as Savior. He vouches for true faith and acts as a down payment until life on this earth is over. One of the many fascinating truths of the Holy Spirit is the way He gently steps in when you don't have the words. In fact, as He does this, sometimes He simply groans, because your thoughts and feelings really are too deep for words.

Lord God, thank You for sending the Holy
Spirit to me! It's a relief to know He'll step in
and intercede even when I have no words.

Listen

Listen to my words, Lord, consider my sighing. Listen to the sound of my cry for help, my King and my God, for to You I pray.

Have you ever noticed it's hard to find a good listener? So many people are fixated on themselves, whether they focus on their own opinions, own experiences, or own feelings. But when you find someone who is interested in your life, asks thoughtful questions to get to know you better, then truly listens to your answers, it's remarkable. You want to spend more time in conversation with a good listener, because it feels good to be known and understood.

Your heavenly Father is the ultimate listener. He gladly hears what you say, whether you're speaking aloud or just thinking. He hears your sighing. He listens to your cries for help. He appreciates your thankfulness when you notice the wonderful things He does. He's genuinely interested in your life, and when you come to Him with absolutely anything, He listens. He knows and understands you more than anyone else ever will.

My King and my God, thank You for knowing me and understanding me. Thank You for listening to my words.

Doing What Feels Unnatural

*"But to you who are listening I say: Love your enemies,
do good to those who hate you, bless those who
curse you, pray for those who mistreat you."*

LUKE 6:27–28 NIV

During Jesus' time on earth, His teachings often were difficult. In fact, to some they might have seemed borderline impossible. Love your enemies? That's a ridiculously hard ask. Do good to those who hate you or bless someone who curses you? That goes against virtually every human feeling or natural response. Pray for those who mistreat you? Following these directions that Jesus gave is uncomfortable and requires you to show undeserved, unmerited kindness.

Yet His directives show how different His teachings are from the world's. Followers of Christ should be different from everyone else, even when they don't give in to typical human nature.

As you look at what Christ taught, look at your prayer life. Instead of holding grudges or complaining about people who mistreat you, do you pray for them? Before you say anything to anyone else, try coming to the Lord in prayer. It will make a huge difference, both in your life and in the life of whoever is mistreating you.

Lord Jesus, it can be hard to obey what You taught!
Please help me do it, even if it seems uncomfortable
to me. When people mistreat me, please help
me do good to them and pray for them.

Success and Mercy

"O Lord, let your ear be attentive to the prayer of your
servant, and to the prayer of your servants who delight to
fear your name, and give success to your servant today,
and grant him mercy in the sight of this man."

NEHEMIAH 1:11 ESV

When the Israelites lived as exiles in Babylon, Nehemiah was cupbearer to the king. A Jew by birth, Nehemiah was heartbroken when he heard that the walls and gates of Jerusalem had been destroyed. He wanted to return to Jerusalem and rebuild the walls, but he had an important job to perform in Babylon. What could he do?

Nehemiah didn't attempt to take matters into his own hands. Before doing anything else, he went directly to the Lord in prayer. His prayer recorded in the first chapter of Nehemiah reveals that he feared the name of the Lord and viewed himself as God's servant. He also knew that God alone could grant success and mercy. After he humbly prayed, he courageously asked the king for permission to return to Jerusalem to rebuild the city's wall. And what happened? The Lord did give Nehemiah both success and mercy.

Father, nothing is too small or too big a matter
for You. I want to ask You for success and
mercy in matters that weigh on my mind.

Spirit and Mind

What am I to do? I will pray with my spirit, but I
will pray with my mind also; I will sing praise with
my spirit, but I will sing with my mind also.

1 CORINTHIANS 14:15 ESV

What are some of your God-given gifts and abilities? The apostle Paul explains many different gifts in 1 Corinthians. In his explanation, Paul points out an important fact: believers need to use both their spirits and their minds when exercising their gifts. And believers need to use both their spirits and minds when praying.

You definitely can pray with your spirit. In fact, sometimes your spirit communicates beyond words. But other times you need to put words to your prayers. You need to pray with your mind and truly think about what you're communicating to the Lord. In other words, as you pray, it's a good idea to pray with both your feelings and your thoughts. Engage both aspects in the way you worship, and watch how much more deeply you'll experience the Lord in your prayers and praise.

Father, thank You for giving me both a mind and a spirit.
I pray I'll use both to worship and communicate with You.

Waiting through Uncertainty

Lord, I call upon You; hurry to me!
Listen to my voice when I call to You!

PSALM 141:1 NASB

Sometimes in life, you may not feel as though God hears your prayers. And other times, you may not feel as though God responds. In fact, you can spend weeks, months, and even years praying about particular requests without seeing any evidence that the Lord is in the middle of answering you. But He always hears, even when you can't see Him moving. He will always respond, even if you can't sense it or even if you forget about your prayers. It's not like you can tap God on the shoulder or look Him in the eye to know that He's paying attention to you.

Many times in prayer, you'll just have to trust His promises and believe that He does know what you're facing. He knows how you feel. And He knows what you need before you even ask. Keep trusting even when you don't see any evidence of change. But when you do notice the way He answers your prayers, be sure to acknowledge His intervention. Thank Him, no matter what His response might be.

> Lord, I can feel so impatient at times. Please help me to wait on You, trusting that You will faithfully answer my prayers. I want to get to know You better in the process.

An Invitation to Rest

*"Come to me, all you who are weary
and burdened, and I will give you rest."*

MATTHEW 11:28 NIV

When Jesus offered rest to His followers, He didn't offer it as an automatic kind of gift. To get Jesus' kind of rest, you need to come to Him first. When you feel weary and worn out by this life, you don't have to carry the weight of your burdens on your own. You can choose to come to Jesus, and when you do, He will give you rest.

Perhaps the most obvious way to come to Jesus is through prayer. Through prayer, you can communicate and open up about anything that seems to be draining you. It's the way you can share what's going on in your life, what you're thinking, how you're processing everything, and what you wish could be different. Through prayer, you can ask for help, strength, energy, time, or any other need. Prayer is the entrance to Jesus' offer of rest. Will you come to Him today?

Lord Jesus, thank You for Your offer of rest! I feel so
tired and exhausted by life at times. I want to come to
You! I want the kind of rest You offer me so freely.

Listening to the Law

If one turns away his ear from hearing the law,
even his prayer is an abomination.

PROVERBS 28:9 ESV

Starting with Moses, God detailed His law as a way to set His people apart through holy living. The Mosaic law specified the Lord's requirements and defined what was right and wrong. Once Jesus came to the world to fulfill the law and create a new covenant, grace entered the picture. But the law didn't disappear forever; in fact, it clearly shows what the Lord desires for His people.

While salvation is a gift of God through faith alone, God's law shouldn't be ignored. The book of Proverbs warns that if you turn away from hearing the law, your prayer will be an abomination. Because you don't want your prayers to be a detestable disgrace, pay attention to God's law. Read the Bible to find out what His law is, and try to honor it. As you do, your prayers will be welcomed.

Lord, I'm grateful that You gave the law to help
guide Your chosen people in right living. Please help
me consider and honor Your law more. I don't want
to turn my ear away from Your commands!

Thankful for Faith

We always thank God, the Father of our Lord Jesus Christ, when
we pray for you, because we have heard of your faith in Christ Jesus
and of the love you have for all God's people—the faith and love
that spring from the hope stored up for you in heaven and about
which you have already heard in the true message of the gospel.

COLOSSIANS 1:3–5 NIV

When you pray for other people, exactly how do you pray for them? Do you stick to requests or focus on current situations you know they're facing? Or do you pray for them because of their faith or hope? When you hear about the way a believer showers others with love, do you thank God for that brother or sister in Christ?

As you notice the really great things other people are doing in faith or out of their love for Christ, don't forget to thank God for them. While you're praying, ask the Lord to bless and strengthen the faith of fellow believers. Celebrate the way God is working in someone else's life. Not only will this honor God and other Christ followers, but it also will be an encouragement to you as you notice God at work in believers' lives.

Father God, thank You for the way You're working
in the lives of so many in Your Church. I pray they'll
be blessed because of their faith and hope in You.
May they reap the rewards of a life full of love.

Waiting for an Answer

Hear, O LORD, when I cry aloud; be gracious to me and answer me!
PSALM 27:7 ESV

Sometimes when you pray, you may feel as if God hears and responds to your every thought, and when He does, it's wonderful! It's such an encouragement to sense God hearing and answering you. But other times He can seem distant. Sometimes it feels like your prayers just come bouncing back from heaven, like you're stuck in an echo chamber listening to yourself. It might feel like you need His response right away, but you're caught in the middle of a waiting game where your patience is forced to grow.

No matter what kind of response you experience, keep praying to your heavenly Father. Cry out to Him in sorrow, in frustration, and in joy. Talk to Him when you're feeling patient and impatient. Don't hold back. Instead, share all that you're thinking and feeling and wondering and wishing. As you do, He'll be gracious to hear you. And if you pay attention, you'll be delighted when He answers you!

Lord, thank You for hearing my prayers! Please help
me wait patiently for Your answer. You're a good, good
God who is always attentive and caring. Thank You!

Alone but Not Alone

Now it happened that as he was praying alone, the disciples were with him. And he asked them, "Who do the crowds say that I am?" And they answered, "John the Baptist. But others say, Elijah, and others, that one of the prophets of old has risen." Then he said to them, "But who do you say that I am?" And Peter answered, "The Christ of God."

LUKE 9:18–20 ESV

During the last few years Jesus was on this earth, His time was filled with public ministry and private discipleship. Surrounded by His twelve closest followers, Jesus spent most of His time in community. While He did get away to pray on His own, sometimes His private prayers happened when His disciples were still with Him.

This kind of commitment to prayer—praying even when surrounded by people—is an excellent example you can follow. Even when life is busy and you feel constantly surrounded by people, you still can pray alone. Not only will your relationship with the Lord grow through these prayers, but you'll also feel refreshed and energized to reach out to the people surrounding you.

Jesus, thank You for the amazing example You lived! Even when other people demanded Your time, energy, and attention, You still made prayer a priority. I want to be just like You and pray!

Praying without Grudges

"As for me, far be it from me that I should sin against the Lord by failing to pray for you. And I will teach you the way that is good and right."

1 SAMUEL 12:23 NIV

In the Old Testament, Israel's prophet, priest, and judge, Samuel, warned the Israelites against making poor choices like selecting a king to rule over them. The Israelites did what they wanted to do, though, and ignored Samuel's counsel. Even after his warnings were ignored, Samuel didn't hold a grudge against the Israelites. In fact, he still prayed for them, and actually considered it a sin against the Lord if he didn't pray for them.

This act of humility and forgiveness is something to emulate. Even when your good advice is ignored, remember Samuel's example and keep praying. Forget about holding a grudge, even when your feelings have been hurt. Continue praying, even if the people you're praying for don't seem to care. Remember that your prayers are to the Lord and you need to continue praying to Him, no matter how others react or respond.

Lord God, thank You for being a God I can pray to on behalf of others. Even if people close to me ignore my advice, I want to be faithful to continue to lift them up in prayer.

Thankful for Others

I thank my God in all my remembrance of you, always in every prayer of mine for you all making my prayer with joy, because of your partnership in the gospel from the first day until now.

PHILIPPIANS 1:3–5 ESV

Who has joined with you in your journey to know and love Christ more? Who has come alongside you to help serve your heavenly Father? As you think about and remember the people God has placed in your life as you pursue and serve Him, thank Him for these sisters and brothers in Christ! As part of the body of Christ, you need other people to function. You simply can't do all the serving and growing on your own.

After you've thanked God, make it a point to thank these people in your life. Everyone loves to feel appreciated and noticed, and everyone could use some encouragement to continue to live out the Gospel.

As you begin to thank God for the people He has blessed you with, you'll find it easier to gratefully notice the good work others do.

Father, I'm so glad I don't have to live the Christian life all by myself! Thank You for surrounding me with a great cloud of believers. And thank You for the way my sisters and brothers in Christ sharpen me and spur me on to love and serve You.

Can You Hear Me?

Give ear to my prayer, O God, and hide
not yourself from my plea for mercy!

PSALM 55:1 ESV

Think of a time when someone completely ignored you. Maybe you were talking away, either pouring your heart out or explaining something in detail, and your spouse or child or coworker didn't pay attention to a single word you said. That probably felt pretty frustrating!

Sometimes you may feel as if God responds the same way to your prayers. You can pray and pray and pray and feel like your words are falling on deaf ears. However, God does listen all the time, even when it doesn't feel like it. He hears every word you pray. And when you're facing a really difficult time, He realizes when you're at the end of your rope and hears you beg for mercy. He knows you and what you're going through. And He loves and cares for you, even when He waits to answer.

Lord, sometimes I get pretty frustrated when You don't seem to hear or care about my prayers. Please comfort me and reassure me that You do listen. I pray You'll listen to every one of my prayers and answer my pleas for mercy. I don't want to face this life without You and Your guidance!

The Power of Faith

*"And whatever you ask in prayer,
you will receive, if you have faith."*

MATTHEW 21:22 ESV

It may be obvious that prayer is a conversation with God. But simply telling the Lord what's on your heart and mind isn't the entirety of prayer. You need faith too. In fact, faith is crucial if you hope to experience any power in prayer.

As Hebrews 11:1 (ESV) explains, "Faith is the assurance of things hoped for, the conviction of things not seen." When you pray to the Lord and ask Him for things in hope and with a conviction that He hears and can answer your prayer, you will receive. The timing and answer may be different than what you expect, but the Lord will faithfully respond to your prayer. As your faith grows and your prayers multiply, you'll watch the Lord answer you in amazing ways.

Father, I'm glad that faith is necessary for prayer. I want
to believe in You and the fact that You can and will do
amazing things. I want my hope in You to grow. I love You!

24

Praise and Confession

I prayed to the LORD my God and confessed, and said, "Oh, Lord, the great and awesome God, who keeps His covenant and faithfulness for those who love Him and keep His commandments, we have sinned, we have done wrong, and acted wickedly and rebelled, even turning aside from Your commandments and ordinances."

DANIEL 9:4–5 NASB

If you've ever tried a formula for praying, you know there are certain prayer patterns that make praying a little easier. For example, the ACTS method includes adoration, confession, thanksgiving, and supplication. Yet there's no single proper way to pray. You certainly are free to pray in any way.

If you're looking for a prayer example, the Bible gives glimpses into the ways various godly men and women prayed. For example, Daniel was known for his prayers. Praise was a large part of Daniel's prayers, as well as confession. When you pray, you can copy his prayers by praising the Lord and confessing any ways you've turned from Him in sin.

Lord Almighty, I praise You because You truly are great and awesome. Thank You for the way You faithfully provide for me in love. Thank You for Your mercy. Please forgive me for the ways I've sinned against You today. I'm sorry I turned away from You. I want to change and follow Your righteous ways.

Praying about Everything

And pray in the Spirit on all occasions with all kinds of
prayers and requests. With this in mind, be alert and
always keep on praying for all the Lord's people.

EPHESIANS 6:18 NIV

When you accept Christ as your Lord and Savior, the Holy Spirit is like your deposit. He vouches for you, fills you, and acts as your seal of assurance. He understands your thoughts, feelings, and groanings.

Because He knows you so intimately, you can and should pray in the Spirit with all kinds of requests. As you go through your day, pay attention to what's happening around you. Be aware of what other people are facing, and then pray for them. And once you pray, keep praying.

Stay alert to the world around you and talk to the Holy Spirit about what you notice with thoughts and words.

Lord, thank You for Your wonderful gift of the Holy Spirit!
I'm thankful He knows me completely. I want to be more
mindful of what's happening around me, and I want to
come to You to pray about anything and everything. Please
help me step up and pray for the people around me!

Worthy of Praise

Shout for joy to God, all the earth; sing the glory of his name; give to him glorious praise! Say to God, "How awesome are your deeds! So great is your power that your enemies come cringing to you."

PSALM 66:1–3 ESV

Everyone likes to know they're appreciated. And knowing that someone adores you can make you feel extra special. When you know someone else notices you, when the things you do are valued, or when the way you do something is prized, you're naturally brought closer to the person who regards you so highly.

Just like you, God loves to know He's noticed and appreciated. Recognizing His power and awesomeness shows you appreciate Him. Of course, God is God and doesn't need anyone's approval or appreciation. But He's also absolutely worthy of praise. When you praise Him in prayer, you consider how wonderful He is while giving Him honor and respect. Praising the Lord will help pull you closer to the King of the universe. You can shout for joy and sing the glory of His name. He is worthy!

Lord God, I praise You! Everything You do is awesome. Your power is both something to fear and something to revere. I praise You for all You've done and all that You can and will do.

Your Gain or the Lord's?

And he was teaching them and saying to them, "Is it not written, 'My house shall be called a house of prayer for all the nations'? But you have made it a den of robbers."

MARK 11:17 ESV

When Jesus was on this earth, He wasn't afraid to point out hypocrisy and sin. He didn't need to curry anyone's favor. Yet He didn't come as a critical judge. He came to teach the truth with complete honesty. And when He noticed the way people at the temple focused on their own gain instead of genuine worship of the Lord, He spoke up.

Just as Jesus spotted greed and distraction at the temple during His earthly life, what would He see if He entered your church today? What would He observe in your life? Would He spy ulterior motives or a heart that's set on worshipping the God of the universe? As you prepare your heart for worship, make sure prayer and reverence are your priorities. Go and make your time at church all about approaching and worshipping the Lord, not about focusing on your own desires and concerns.

Father, I've sinned against You when I've made church all about me and my own gain or preferences. Please forgive me. I want to worship You in Your holy place with a whole heart.

The Humility of Prayer

"If my people, who are called by my name, will humble themselves and pray and seek my face and turn from their wicked ways, then I will hear from heaven, and I will forgive their sin and will heal their land."

2 CHRONICLES 7:14 NIV

One important quality of prayer is the aspect of humility. When you pray, you're humbly admitting that God is the all-powerful God and you're not. You don't have control over situations, but He does. You can't change a person's heart, but He can.

If you're chosen by Him and called by His name, praying involves laying down your own agenda and pride and asking God to work.

When you pray, you turn away from yourself and to the Lord. And instead of seeking His hand to find out what He's doing, humble prayer involves seeking God's face, or knowing who God is. Your prayers are filled with worship and focus on the God of the universe instead of yourself and your issues. When prayer is filled with this kind of humility, God hears and forgives and heals.

Lord God, I humbly bow before You in worship.
You are so great and worthy of all praise. I
want to know You more deeply. I'm so grateful
that when I seek You, You will be found!

A Good Partnership

I pray that your partnership with us in the faith may
be effective in deepening your understanding of every
good thing we share for the sake of Christ.

PHILEMON 1:6 NIV

Partners are such a good gift. Whether in business, ministry, marriage, or simply friendship, uniting with someone else over a common interest is wonderful. Having a partner in the faith is especially valuable. Instead of trying to live the Christian life alone, you can encourage a fellow believer—and be encouraged.

As you connect with other believers and find a few you can especially relate to, don't be afraid to open up and share what's on your heart and mind. Be honest about your strengths and struggles. Discuss what you're reading in the Bible and figure out how scripture intersects with your lives. As you do, you'll deepen your understanding and help each other strengthen your walks with Christ.

Father, thank You for the good gift of partners! Help me
choose my confidants wisely, then step out and honestly
share what's going on in my mind and heart. Please help
me be a very good friend. And please bring a very good
friend into my life. Use us to point each other to You.

Praise Him

*You, Lord, are forgiving and good, abounding
in love to all who call to you.*

PSALM 86:5 NIV

When you stop and ponder the Lord, what's the first thought that comes to mind?

He's the sovereign God who created all things. He's all-powerful and holds all things together. He's all-knowing and always and forever present. His ways are higher than your ways, and His thoughts are higher than your thoughts. His grace runs deep, and He's infinitely kind. He's just and jealous, full of mercy and wisdom. He's unchangeable and holy. As an eternal and timeless God, He's the Beginning and the End. He forgives when He has been wronged, and He is very, very good. He abounds in love and is absolute truth.

Realizing all these qualities is enough to make any person bow in worship. Have you stopped to praise the Maker of heaven and earth today? Have you stopped to call to Him?

Lord, You are amazing! Your goodness is unfathomable,
and I worship You. What a blessing that I can
know and trust You, the one true God. You are
worthy of all glory and honor and praise.

Drawn to Jesus

Then people brought little children to Jesus for him to place his hands on them and pray for them. But the disciples rebuked them. Jesus said, "Let the little children come to me, and do not hinder them, for the kingdom of heaven belongs to such as these." When he had placed his hands on them, he went on from there.

MATTHEW 19:13–15 NIV

When Jesus lived on this earth, He drew so many people to Himself. Did He have a magnetic personality? Could people tell something was different about Him? Could people quickly figure out He was the Son of God? Whatever it was, men, women, and children, the sick, dying, demon-possessed, blind, deaf, and lame came to Jesus.

Sometimes, surprised by the people seeking attention, Jesus' disciples weren't the most welcoming bunch. But Jesus wasn't like them. He welcomed everyone with love and compassion.

The wonderful news is that nothing has changed. Just as He didn't want to hinder anyone from coming to Him, Jesus is waiting for you to come to Him with your prayers. No request or concern is too big or too small for Him.

Lord Jesus, thank You for Your willingness to listen to me and for Your amazing love and mercy. Your goodness is so different from what I find in this world. I'm eternally thankful for You and Your loving-kindness.

Ponder in Prayer

Then he prayed to the Lord and said, "Please Lord, was this not what I said when I was still in my own country? Therefore in anticipation of this I fled to Tarshish, since I knew that You are a gracious and compassionate God, slow to anger and abundant in mercy, and One who relents of disaster."

JONAH 4:2 NASB

When the Lord told Jonah to warn the Ninevites about the consequences of their sins, Jonah fled—and ended up in the belly of a fish as a result. Once the fish spit Jonah out, he headed to Nineveh to do exactly what the Lord asked—and the Ninevites repented!

Afterward, Jonah talked to God. To process what he experienced, he summarized and pondered everything in a prayer.

Just like Jonah, you may have a big milestone or adventure to ponder—hopefully it doesn't involve being swallowed alive! Go ahead and talk everything over with God. Even though He knows every detail, He's happy to listen to what you have to say about matters. Openly share what's on your mind, including the good, the bad, and the truths you learned about God during your experience. Summarize what has happened and then share it all: what you've realized, what disappointed you, and what brought you hope.

Lord, sometimes the best thing to do is talk through things to process all my thoughts and feelings. I'm so thankful You're a gracious and compassionate God who is always willing to listen to me!

Joining Together in Prayer

They all joined together constantly in prayer, along with the women and Mary the mother of Jesus, and with his brothers.

ACTS 1:14 NIV

After Christ rose from the dead, showed Himself to hundreds of people, then ascended into heaven, the early church met often. In fact, they were an ultimate picture of living life together. One of their main trademarks was their commitment to prayer.

They joined together in prayer, not just when they felt like it and not just every now and then. They all joined together in prayer constantly.

Praying to God was one of their top priorities, and it proved helpful for every single situation. Prayer helped the early believers get closer to God. In the process, God knit their hearts together and gave them insight and understanding as well as plenty of blessings.

As with the early church, joining together in prayer with other believers will go a long way in building your relationship with the Lord and each other. The more constantly you do pray, the better!

Lord God, thank You for the example of the early church. Through their commitment to You and love for You, they teach me how to better relate to You. I want to pray to You so much more. Please help me be more consistent in my prayers to You.

Mercy!

Praise be to the LORD, for he has heard my cry for mercy.
PSALM 28:6 NIV

Sometimes life's situations can overwhelm you. Just when one thing goes wrong, an entire snowball effect seems to begin, and catastrophe after catastrophe keeps happening. When you're stuck in a cycle of heart-wrenching, painful events and situations, it's natural to feel stressed and distraught. In those moments, it's easy to realize you've come to the end of yourself. You have nothing left to offer or do to make things better. You're powerless and you know it.

When the weight of despair comes crashing down, you eventually reach a point when you need to cry out for mercy. In your ugliest, most desperate moments, the Lord is there, waiting to help. And when you finally realize absolutely everything is out of your control, it's easy to remember who truly is in control. He has the power to lift you up out of the pit of despair. He can make all things right. As you surrender everything to the Author and Perfecter of your faith, you can cry out for His mercy. He'll hear and respond.

Father, I praise You for hearing my cry for mercy
and for being ready and willing to respond. I don't
know what I'd do without You in my life!

Answered Prayers

But the angel said to him, "Do not be afraid, Zechariah,
for your prayer has been heard, and your wife Elizabeth
will bear you a son, and you shall name him John."

LUKE 1:13 NASB

God is in the business of hearing and answering prayers. In fact, He always has been. Before Jesus was born, Zechariah was a devout priest who was childless. The burden of a lifetime without fatherhood weighed heavily on him, and he did exactly what he should: bring all his thoughts and concerns and requests to the Lord. But God surprised Zechariah in a few ways: not only did the Lord send an angel to talk with him, but the angel also promised elderly Zechariah that he would have a son.

God had heard Zechariah's prayers, and just when it seemed as if He wouldn't answer, God surprised Zechariah, his wife, Elizabeth, and all their acquaintances with something completely unlikely: a baby boy!

Even when it seems as if God will never answer your prayers, keep praying. He hears you!

Lord, thank You for the way You hear prayers and
the way You answer them. Even if I can't understand
the timing or purpose of Your answers, You have
a specific purpose, and for that I'm grateful.

The God Who Hears and Sees

Then the word of the LORD came to Isaiah: "Go and tell Hezekiah, 'This is what the LORD, the God of your father David, says: I have heard your prayer and seen your tears; I will add fifteen years to your life.'"

ISAIAH 38:4–5 NIV

When you pray, sometimes it's easy to forget that the God of the universe is listening to every word. He hears your requests. He sees the tears you cry. He knows the situations and fears you face. Even when you're pouring out your heart to Him and He seems silent, He really is there. He really does hear you.

In the Old Testament, the prophet Isaiah told King Hezekiah that his sickness would end in death. Hezekiah was so distraught he "turned his face to the wall and prayed to the LORD" and "wept bitterly" (Isaiah 38:2–3 NIV). The Lord heard his prayer and added fifteen years to his life, much to Hezekiah's delight and surprise.

Hezekiah's response? He prayed again, full of praise and humility. When you realize the Lord hears and answers your prayers, make sure to praise and thank Him. He's worthy of all your praise!

Lord God, You are so good to those who love and honor You. Even when You don't answer my prayers the way I hoped, I want to continue to seek You and praise You, no matter what.

Working on a To-Do List

But you, beloved, building yourselves up in your most holy faith and praying in the Holy Spirit, keep yourselves in the love of God, waiting for the mercy of our Lord Jesus Christ that leads to eternal life.

JUDE 1:20–21 ESV

As a helpful way to keep track of obligations and plans, to-do lists are a normal part of life. This is nothing new; many of the epistles in the New Testament are filled with imperative commands—basically, to-do lists for the Christian life.

Jude encouraged believers that as they kept themselves in the love of God and waited for Christ's mercy, they should build themselves up in their most holy faith and pray in the Holy Spirit.

If you need to find a focus for your day, keep building your faith and praying! Prayer is an excellent partner to a life of faith.

Lord, thank You for Your love and mercy! Please
help my faith in You grow. May my prayers to
You help strengthen and build my faith.

Any Time of the Day

As for me, I shall call upon God, and the LORD will
save me. Evening and morning and at noon, I will
complain and moan, and He will hear my voice.

PSALM 55:16–17 NASB

When life is hard and you're going through awful situations, it's easy
to focus on your problems. After all, when you feel weighed down or
burdened by trials, it's hard to stop thinking about them.

The psalmist experienced the same kind of thoughts. But as he
dwelled on his complaints, he did something about them: he prayed.
As Psalm 55 details, he called upon the Lord to complain and moan in
the evening, in the morning, and at noon. All day and all night long,
whenever his problems came to mind, he prayed because he knew the
Lord would hear his prayers and save him.

What an encouragement to know that even when you're walking
through the toughest moments, you can tell the Lord all your frustra-
tions and fears at any time of the day.

> Lord, even if no one else in this world understands
> what I'm going through, You're faithful to listen
> to me and my complaints. Please fill me with
> peace as I wait for You to right my wrongs.

Love and Pray for. . .Who?!

"You have heard that it was said, 'You shall love your neighbor and hate your enemy.' But I say to you, love your enemies and pray for those who persecute you."

MATTHEW 5:43–44 NASB

When Jesus encountered people during His life on earth, He often surprised them by His parables and teachings. For example, a natural response is to love those who love you and hate people who hate you. But Jesus lived a life of love and astounded His followers when He told them to love others regardless of how they were treated.

You should love those who love you and love those who hate you; in other words, love both your friends and your enemies. Hatred of any kind has no place in Jesus' teachings.

Along with showing unconditional love, Jesus taught His followers to pray for their persecutors. Just as it's easy to love those who love you, it's also easy to pray for the people closest to you. Yet Jesus calls His followers to pray for their opposition. While it's not easy, this life of love and prayer should become the trademark of every Christ follower.

Jesus, You lived a life of love! I want to be like You. Please help me to love and pray for others, whether they love me or hate me.

A Proper Perspective

"Nevertheless, turn Your attention to the prayer of Your servant and to his plea, LORD, my God, to listen to the cry and to the prayer which Your servant prays before You today, so that Your eyes may be open toward this house night and day, toward the place of which You have said, 'My name shall be there,' to listen to the prayer which Your servant will pray toward this place."

1 KINGS 8:28–29 NASB

King Solomon was one of the wisest men ever to live, yet even with his riches and fame and power, he still knew how to humble himself before the Lord. Even though he was king of the Israelites, Solomon considered himself the Lord's servant. It wasn't beneath him to plead to the Lord.

As Solomon dedicated the Lord's temple, he recognized God's immense greatness. As he prayed, Solomon knew he was in the presence of God. He knew how to pray with honor and reverence.

While the Lord is your Shepherd and would love for you to bring all your brutally honest prayers to Him, He still is King of kings and Lord of lords. He deserves all your genuine praise, sincere honor, and humble adoration.

Lord God, You truly are great. I worship You as Lord of heaven and earth. Thank You for listening to my prayers.

Night and Day

*How can we thank God enough for you in return for all
the joy we have in the presence of our God because of you?
Night and day we pray most earnestly that we may see
you again and supply what is lacking in your faith.*

1 Thessalonians 3:9–10 NIV

When someone holds a special place in your heart, you can't help but think about that person. You want to spend time together and look forward to opportunities to talk and connect in person. It doesn't matter if this person is a friend, family member, coworker, fellow servant, or romantic interest. When you care about someone else, you experience joy and you want the best for that person.

The apostle Paul put these feelings into words as he wrote to the Thessalonian church. He thanked God for the believers in Thessalonica and prayed to see his friends again.

When you're a believer, praying for people who are on your mind and in your heart comes naturally—even at all hours of the night and day. Prayer is a powerful force. It makes a difference!

Father God, I'm glad I can talk with You about the people
I love most. Please work in their lives and strengthen their
faith so they come to know and love You more and more.

Calling Out to God

In my distress I called to the LORD; I cried to my God for help. From his temple he heard my voice; my cry came before him, into his ears.

If you're hurt or trapped or sense danger, what's a natural response? Calling out for help! It doesn't matter if you're all alone, with people you know, or surrounded by a sea of strangers: calling for help is an immediate reaction.

When you know you're in distress—maybe you're physically in danger or mentally feeling devastated or distraught—finding a person to help you is a good course of action. But coming to the Lord for help is of the utmost importance. When you're in distress, you can call out to Him. You can cry to Him for help with anything.

If you feel too embarrassed or vulnerable to reveal your deepest secrets to another person, go ahead and confess them to your heavenly Father. He already knows them anyway, but it can be a huge relief to get things off your chest. When you do cry out to Him, He'll hear and be quick to respond in some way.

> Father, thank You for being my Help! Thank You
> for always being available and ready to listen. No
> matter how big or small my issues are, I know
> I can trust You with absolutely anything.

Strength

"But I have prayed for you, that your faith will not fail; and you, when you have turned back, strengthen your brothers."

LUKE 22:32 NASB

Life is hard. Granted, not every single part of life is difficult, and joy can be part of every day. But difficult times come to every single person. It's not a matter of *if* you will face trials but *when* you will face them. Enduring and persevering takes an enormous amount of effort, energy, and faith.

As you face difficulties, pray that your faith will stay strong. When it feels like your faith is faltering, remind yourself of your belief in the Lord. Remember the faithful, gracious way He loves and cares for you. Pray to Him and ask Him to strengthen your faith.

Once you've passed through your battle, encourage and strengthen other believers. Especially when you notice others facing hard times, pray for them. You can offer to help and encourage them in generous, practical ways, but don't forget them in prayer. Bringing your requests to the Lord will do more good than you realize.

Father, please give me strength as I face hard times!
And please strengthen my sisters and brothers
who are walking through trials right now.

Praying without Profit

"They say to God, 'Depart from us! We do not desire the knowledge of your ways. What is the Almighty, that we should serve him? And what profit do we get if we pray to him?'"

JOB 21:14–15 ESV

The book of Job is an interesting look into the way a godly man suffered and how he and others responded to his immense trials. Even as he lived through more pain than most people can imagine, he still kept a clear picture of the Lord and life.

Job knew the wicked wanted absolutely nothing to do with God. They didn't want to learn about a godly way of life, they didn't want to imagine serving the Lord, and they didn't believe they'd gain anything by praying to him. Job wasn't wicked though. He knew the tremendous blessings that came from serving the Almighty. And even in his pain and tribulations, he continued praying to the Lord.

His prayers were an act of faith even in the middle of his suffering. Through his prayers, Job reminded himself of the powerful truth that God was and is perfectly just. Likewise, when you face trials and hardships, keep praying not as a way to profit, but as a way to communicate with and praise your Maker.

> Lord God, I don't need to come to You in
> prayer to profit in any way. I want to come to
> You today to worship and serve You.

Praying for Specifics

*Finally, brothers and sisters, pray for us that the word
of the Lord will spread rapidly and be glorified, just as
it was also with you; and that we will be rescued from
troublesome and evil people; for not all have the faith.*

2 THESSALONIANS 3:1–2 NASB

When you pray, sometimes you have no words. You feel plenty of
emotions but can't seem to describe everything you're feeling. Other
times you know exactly what you want to pray about. People have given
you very specific requests, or you're aware of details and begin praying
about them. Both kinds of prayers are excellent!

The Holy Spirit intercedes for you when you have no words, and the
Lord listens to wordy, specific prayers too. The apostle Paul is a great
example of a man who wasn't afraid to ask people to pray for specific
requests. He asked his friends and fellow believers in Thessalonica to
pray for three things: that the Word of the Lord would spread rapidly,
that the Word of the Lord would be glorified, and that he and his men
would be rescued from troublesome, evil people. Instead of making a
generic request like "Please pray for me," he gave believers a chance to
ask and trust God for specific details.

Father, You're a God of details. I want to trust You
for the littlest things as well as the big picture.

46

Praying in Faith

Hear my prayer, LORD! And let my cry for help come to You. Do not hide Your face from me on the day of my distress; incline Your ear to me; on the day when I call answer me quickly.

PSALM 102:1–2 NASB

As much as prayer is direct communication with God, it might not always feel like it. Sometimes you can pray and pray and pray, but in the middle of praying, you feel doubt creep into your mind. *Does God hear me? Does He listen to my cry for help? When I'm in trouble, will He rescue me?* But thinking of prayer as merely a two-way communication cycle of talking and answering misses out on a vital component: faith.

When you pray in faith, everything changes. You have faith that God does hear you. You have faith that He listens and will respond. You have faith that He will answer you when you call. As the book of Hebrews explains, "Now faith is confidence in what we hope for and assurance about what we do not see. This is what the ancients were commended for" (11:1–2 NIV). When you pray in faith, you put your confidence in the Lord. He'll commend you for your faith in Him.

Lord God, I put my faith fully in You! Thank You for hearing my prayers and responding to me in Your great love and mercy.

Pray and Praise

Is anyone among you in trouble? Let them pray.
Is anyone happy? Let them sing songs of praise.

JAMES 5:13 NIV

James, the half brother of Jesus, wrote a lot of specific details about prayer. First of all, he explained that you can and should pray in any situation. If and when you're in trouble, pray! At the lowest points of your life, when you feel helpless or hopeless, take all your thoughts and concerns and requests to the Lord in prayer.

And in opposite situations, in those good times when you're happy, praise the Lord! You can praise the Lord by praying to Him and singing to Him.

Whatever situation or mood you're dealing with, pray. Bring your thoughts and emotions to the Lord. Praise Him in good times and seek His help and wisdom in difficult times.

Father, I'm so thankful I can come to You in absolutely
any situation. You won't turn me away if I'm experiencing
difficulty. Thanks for welcoming me and for lovingly
listening to me no matter what's happening.

Praying for the Sick

Is anyone among you sick? Let them call the elders of the church to pray over them and anoint them with oil in the name of the Lord.

JAMES 5:14 NIV

After James told believers to pray in all circumstances—with our problems and our praise—he went on to explain the importance of sharing our burdens with other believers so they can pray with us and for us. Specifically, James gave instructions for church elders: they need to pray over and anoint the sick in the name of the Lord.

If you're sick or feeling unwell today, have you shared your situation with anyone else? Has anyone joined you in prayer? Naturally you can pray for yourself and your health. You can and should pray for others who are sick and ask other believers to pray for your health. But you also need to take the added step of bringing your health concerns to your local church. Call the elders of your church and ask them to pray for you. In doing so, you'll be able to experience the blessings of prayer and let others experience them too.

Father, I don't always want to share my health details with other people. So You will be glorified, though, please help me find trusted believers to pray with me. And please help me find comfort as I go to the church for prayer.

Faith and Forgiveness

And the prayer offered in faith will make the sick person well; the Lord will raise them up. If they have sinned, they will be forgiven.

JAMES 5:15 NIV

James specified that those who are sick should invite others into their experience to pray for them. But why? According to James, it has a lot to do with faith and forgiveness. When you invite elders of the church to come and pray over you and your sickness, they'll pray in faith. James says prayers offered in faith will make the sick well.

Moreover, any time that you pray for health is an opportune time to examine your life for sin. How have you sinned? What habitual sin patterns are in your life? What do you need to confess? Do you need to repent and turn from sin? As you confess and repent, you'll experience the freedom that comes from the Lord's forgiveness.

Father God, as I confess my sins to you now, I pray that You'll forgive me. And, as I believe in faith that You can heal me from my sickness, I pray You will heal me.

The Importance of Confession

*Therefore confess your sins to each other and pray
for each other so that you may be healed. The prayer
of a righteous person is powerful and effective.*

JAMES 5:16 NIV

Typically confessions aren't very easy. In fact, knowing you've done something wrong and need to own up to that sin is pretty uncomfortable.

Putting comfort aside, confession is a necessary part of life. When you wrong someone or do something wrong, you need to take ownership for it, recognize it was wrong, then ask forgiveness. When you finish that difficult, uncomfortable process, you'll experience freedom as your conscience is cleared.

In his instructions about prayer, James adds that once we confess our sins, we need to pray for each other. When we honestly share our lives with others through confession and prayer, change will begin. As James explains, when someone is right with God, their prayers are powerful and effective. That's the kind of prayer each one of us would like to have!

Father, even when it's uncomfortable to admit I'm wrong,
I pray I'll be quick to do it. Please forgive my sins and
help me make right choices so I might live a righteous
life. I love You and want to honor You with my life!

The Power of a Righteous Prayer

*Elijah was a man with a nature like ours, and he prayed
earnestly that it would not rain, and it did not rain on the
earth for three years and six months. Then he prayed again,
and the sky poured rain and the earth produced its fruit.*

JAMES 5:17–18 NASB

James concludes his teachings on prayer with a real-life, biblical example. After saying that the prayer of a righteous person is powerful and effective, James gives the example of Elijah. Elijah was just a man, but he was righteous. In fact, he was a righteous man who prayed earnestly. As a result of his serious, forthright prayers offered in faith, God answered him. After Elijah prayed for the Lord to withhold rain, it didn't rain for three and a half years! Then, when Elijah prayed for the Lord to send rain, God answered and showers watered the earth.

As you ponder Elijah's example, how can you personally grow in righteousness? How can you expand your personal trust in the Lord? What can you pray for with complete faith in the Lord?

Lord, please increase my faith in You! And please show
me how my life can become more righteous in Your sight.
I want to trust and believe You for really big things.

Getting Away to Pray

And after saying goodbye to them, He left for the mountain to pray.
MARK 6:46 NASB

Sometimes it's tempting to stay right where you are and power through your everyday life. Tasks need to be completed and people need your attention. But when you're tempted to go, go, go and do, do, do, consider Jesus.

Jesus knew His time on earth was limited. He had plenty of tasks He could do, and throngs of people sought His attention. Yet Jesus didn't try to do it all. He didn't keep going at all hours of the day and night to increase His productivity. What He did do was regularly get away from the demands and crowds to pray by Himself without distractions. Prayer was a huge priority for Him.

What would your life look like if you made prayer a priority? If you could regularly get away to pray, what difference could it make in the way you live?

Lord Jesus, thank You for modeling the importance
of getting away to pray. Please help me make
prayer a priority so I can get to know You better
and reflect You to the world around me.

53

Bloom Where You're Planted

"Seek the prosperity of the city where I have sent you into exile, and pray to the Lord in its behalf; for in its prosperity will be your prosperity."

When the people of Israel found themselves in exile in a foreign land, no doubt their circumstances easily could have led them to be depressed. It wouldn't have been unreasonable for them to hold a grudge or throw pity party after pity party. Yet through Jeremiah the prophet, the Lord asked them to respond in a very different way: to seek the prosperity of Babylon and pray to the Lord on its behalf.

Instead of wanting the worst for the land of their captivity, the Israelites were asked to pray for the best. Babylon's prosperity would be their prosperity.

In much the same way, sometimes in life you're put in situations you'd rather avoid. Sometimes you need to live somewhere you'd rather not live. In those moments, it's easy to complain and wish your situation away. Instead of holding a grudge and wallowing in discontentment, though, try praying for the place where you live or the environment in which you find yourself. Pray for the best, and see how your attitude might change.

Father, thank You for putting me right where You want me. Please help me bloom where You've planted me.

Praying for Salvation

Brothers and sisters, my heart's desire and my prayer to God for them is for their salvation.

ROMANS 10:1 NASB

One of the greatest prayers and concerns for a person's life is salvation—being saved from the penalty of sin. This deliverance from death comes from Christ alone.

As vital as salvation is in determining eternal life or eternal death, not everyone is saved. As a result, believers in Christ need to pray for the salvation or rescue of unbelievers.

God alone can save through Christ. As Acts 4:12 (NIV) explains, "Salvation is found in no one else, for there is no other name under heaven given to mankind by which we must be saved." If you know this way to salvation is true, it's time to begin praying for the salvation of the unbelievers in your life. Who can you pray for, that they might be rescued from eternal punishment and separation from God? How can you begin to look at someone else's salvation as your heart's desire and prayer to God?

Father God, You have the power to change hearts and You have the power to save. I want to pray more often for my loved ones who haven't chosen to follow You yet. Please work in their lives and hearts so they might experience Your salvation!

Hear! Listen! Answer!

Hear my prayer, LORD, listen to my pleadings! Answer me in Your faithfulness, in Your righteousness!

PSALM 143:1 NASB

When you're passionate about something in particular, it's natural to pray with passion too. You can and should plead with the Lord. Pray and pray and pray. Ask Him to answer your prayers. Remind yourself of the Lord's qualities, such as His faithfulness and righteousness. He's loving. He's kind. He's full of mercy. You can and should thank Him for these attributes. You can and should ask Him to act on your behalf.

As you pour out your heart to the Lord in prayer, you also can recognize that your prayers are a sincere way to personally worship the Lord of heaven and earth. Bring your requests to Him, and praise Him too.

Lord, You are so good! Your love endures forever.
You're faithful to Your promises and You're
faithful to me. Your righteousness is perfect. I pray
You'll hear my prayers. Please answer me!

Trading the Hustle

But Jesus often withdrew to lonely places and prayed.
LUKE 5:16 NIV

Withdrawing from the world to spend time alone isn't something that's typically encouraged in today's culture. Messages to hustle and work hard to crush your goals are communicated over and over. Yet all hustling does is wear you out. And when you're exhausted from striving and straining to achieve what feels just out of your reach, you're left feeling empty instead of fulfilled.

Out of anyone, Jesus had a reason to hustle. He was sent to earth on a rescue mission. He alone could heal and teach and save like no one else. But He didn't spend His three years of public ministry overwhelming or exhausting Himself. Instead, He often withdrew to lonely places to pray. Instead of rushing into the crowds of people who desperately wanted and needed Him, He retreated.

The next time you feel tempted to conquer your goals and do it all, try withdrawing instead. Pray instead of perform. Then watch what the Lord will do as a result of your time of prayer.

> Lord Jesus, I want to be more like You! Please
> help me follow Your lead and withdraw to
> pray. You alone can refresh my soul!

Finding Courage to Pray

*"For you, my God, have revealed to your servant
that you will build a house for him. Therefore your
servant has found courage to pray before you."*

1 CHRONICLES 17:25 ESV

When the Lord reveals good news or a specific promise to you, it can
be so encouraging and invigorating. For one thing, you're reminded
that the Lord of all creation really does know you. He really does have
a special plan for your life. Being reminded of the way God sees and
knows you gives you more courage to pray.

While prayer seems like a simple matter, it can feel overwhelming
if you aren't sure what to say or aren't sure if God is even listening to
you. Once you know He is listening and He does care, you can grow
in courage to pray about anything. Once you've found courage to pray
before Him, don't stop doing it! Keep praying and praising Him.

Father, I do praise You for being Lord of all. Sometimes
I struggle to believe You really care about me and
really hear my prayers. Please affirm Your presence
in my life. Please show me that You care about
what's on my heart and my mind. Please show me
the way You're working in my life. Thank You!

Praying for Others

Now we pray to God that you will not do anything wrong—not so that people will see that we have stood the test but so that you will do what is right even though we may seem to have failed.

2 CORINTHIANS 13:7 NIV

When you've invested yourself in someone else's life, you want to watch them grow in strength and success. You care deeply for them and hope for the best for them. You want them to choose what's right and turn away from what's wrong. Regardless of how their success or failure reflects on you, you truly just want to know this person so dear to you has chosen what's right.

Of course, you're not responsible for the path someone else chooses. You're only responsible and accountable for your own decisions. But you certainly can pray for someone else's choices and growth. You can pray that the ones you love will choose to do what is right.

Lord God, thank You for bringing others into my life for me to love, care for, and shepherd. I pray for the direction of their lives right now. Please help them turn from what's wrong and choose what's right. Please remind them of Your truth, and convict them to honor You with their lives and choices.

Give Us Success!

Save us, we pray, O LORD! O LORD, we pray, give us success!
PSALM 118:25 ESV

Most likely, you hope to be successful in what you do. Not many people set out to fail. But how often are you honest with yourself about how much you'd really like to experience success? Whether you desire to experience thriving, fulfilling relationships or to see the work you do flourish and prosper, you hope your faithful efforts will result in fruitfulness. Yet in the middle of all your effort, do you ask the Lord for success as much as you could?

The psalmist very openly prayed for the Lord to give success. Just as this cry for success was appropriate for the Israelites, it's appropriate for you too. Ask God to save you and give you success. Keep working diligently. Then watch what the Lord will do through your effort and prayers.

Oh Lord, would You please give me success? I'd love to watch You work in my life and in my work in awe-inspiring ways. Please help my success bring honor to Your name.

Praying for Help

And he said to them, "The harvest is plentiful, but the laborers are few. Therefore pray earnestly to the Lord of the harvest to send out laborers into his harvest."

LUKE 10:2 ESV

Have you ever heard of the Pareto principle? Supposedly twenty percent of the people do eighty percent of the work. You can see this principle in motion in any organization. You may be part of the tired twenty percent juggling the majority of the work.

This unbalanced division of labor isn't anything new. Jesus knew the laborers are few. In fact, He knew that many people were ready to respond to His Good News—but not many people were ready, willing, or available to take that Good News to the masses.

Instead of getting frustrated by the weighty responsibility, we can be thankful Jesus also presented a solution: prayer. So you don't get stuck doing most of the work, pray that the Lord will send out other workers and helpers. Pray that you won't need to labor alone or feel overworked.

Father, please send other workers to help me! And please help me find other believers I can partner with to bring Your Good News to this world.

The Time Is Now

Seek the LORD while He may be found;
call upon Him while He is near.

ISAIAH 55:6 NASB

Gardening is rooted and grounded by seasons. There are specific times to plant, let plants grow, harvest, then let the ground rest. It's impossible to harvest the fruit of your labor if it's planting time. And when the ground is resting and dormant, it's unreasonable to expect to see any sort of growth.

Just as there are specific times in gardening, the Lord has specific times too. The prophet Isaiah encouraged others to seek the Lord while He may be found. In other words, a time will come when you won't be able to seek Him.

Similarly, you're encouraged to call upon Him while He is near. This calling upon the Lord is an encouragement to pray, and to pray now. Right now is the season to seek Him and call upon Him. Seek and pray while you can.

> Lord God, I don't want to take You for granted, and I
> don't want to take the miracle and blessing of prayer
> for granted either. Now, while I have breath in my
> lungs, I want to seek You. I want to call upon You.

All People

I urge, then, first of all, that petitions, prayers, intercession
and thanksgiving be made for all people—for kings
and all those in authority, that we may live peaceful
and quiet lives in all godliness and holiness.
1 Timothy 2:1–2 NIV

In this world, it can feel really difficult to pray for certain people. Praying for your enemies and for people who have hurt you can be a challenge. It also can feel tough to pray for those in authority, especially if you don't agree with them.

Yet the Bible is clear: you need to pray for everyone. You need to thank the Lord for all people: both those you appreciate and those you don't. You need to intercede through prayer for all people: both those you love to spend time with and those you don't. You need to petition the King of kings and Lord of lords for all people: both those you adore and those you don't.

As you do begin to pray for all people, your life will change. You'll become godlier and holier in the process, and your life will radiate peace as you trust and obey the Lord.

Father God, even when I don't feel like praying for specific people in my life, compel me to do it anyway. I want to be more like You, and in doing this, I can. I love You!

He Hears You!

The LORD has heard my pleading,
the LORD receives my prayer.
PSALM 6:9 NASB

When you feel so passionately about something that you plead to someone, you're not complacent. You're invested in the outcome. You desperately want something. And in that desperation and passion, you want to know that the person you're petitioning is paying attention. It's unbelievably frustrating to pour out your heart and make a plea, only to realize that no one listened to you.

When you pour out your heart to the Lord and bring your plea to Him, you can't expect to hear an audible answer. But He hears. He receives your prayer. His Word promises that He does and, in faith, you can trust His promises. Even if you don't hear His voice, you can witness the ways He'll answer your prayers throughout your life. Watch for the ways He's at work. Pay attention to the ways He responds to your pleading.

Lord, I choose to trust and believe the truth of Your
Word. Even if I can't hear You, I know You hear my
pleading and receive my prayer. Thank You!

Ask with Belief

*"Therefore I tell you, whatever you ask in prayer,
believe that you have received it, and it will be yours."*

MARK 11:24 ESV

Jesus lived a life of prayer, and He taught His followers about prayer too. According to Jesus, faith and belief profoundly affect your prayers. Do you believe what you're praying?

English preacher Charles Spurgeon taught that Mark 11:24 describes the miracle of faith: "Ye cannot pray so as to be heard in heaven and answered to your soul's satisfaction, unless you believe that God really hears and will answer you."

When you're praying, honestly ask the Lord for those things within His will that you long to see come to pass. Then believe in the power of prayer. Don't just count prayer as something you've done that hopefully might work. Count it for what it really is: you're telling the God of the universe exactly what you want, so far as it is in line with His will, and you're trusting His power and truly believing He'll answer your prayer.

Can belief feel elusive sometimes? Of course. But belief in God's power and providence is absolutely necessary.

Father God, please forgive me for my unbelief.
I choose to believe in You and the powerful
way You work in this world and in my life.

He Can Be Found

"Then you will call upon Me and come and pray to Me,
and I will listen to you. And you will seek Me and find
Me when you search for Me with all your heart."

JEREMIAH 29:12–13 NASB

Through the prophet Jeremiah, the Lord promised beautiful truths for His followers: He will hear you when you call upon Him. He will listen when you come and pray to Him. He will be found when you seek and search for Him.

How wonderful that the God of the universe is willing to be found! How wonderful that He is willing to listen!

His promises are conditional though. They depend on you. Will you call upon Him? Will you come to Him? Will you pray to Him? Will you seek Him? Will you search for Him with all your heart? When you do, He'll respond with love and mercy and kindness.

> Father, You are so very good to me! What a special
> gift that when I call upon You and pray, You listen.
> How amazing that when I truly search for You with
> all my heart, You are found. You don't stay hidden.
> You are never aloof and standoffish. Thank You!

Three Not-So-Simple Instructions

Rejoice always, pray without ceasing, give thanks in all circumstances; for this is the will of God in Christ Jesus for you.

1 THESSALONIANS 5:16–18 ESV

The apostle Paul's teaching to the Thessalonian church seems simple enough: Rejoice. Pray. Give thanks. When you do these three things, you're doing the will of God.

But these three commands aren't necessarily easy when you notice the details. When should you rejoice? Always—when life is going great and you feel like it *and* when things are going wrong and you don't feel like rejoicing. How should you pray? Without ceasing—that's continual prayer woven throughout your entire day. And when should you give thanks? In all circumstances, both good and bad, when things are confusing and when they are crystal clear. Always rejoice. Never stop praying. And give thanks in every situation.

Father, sometimes my attitude isn't very good.
It's hard for me to rejoice always, especially when
I don't feel like rejoicing. Sometimes I forget to
pray. And other times I just don't feel like being
thankful. Please transform my heart so I can be more
consistent in rejoicing, praying, and thanking You.

What's Your Motive?

*Hear a just cause, LORD, give Your attention to my cry;
listen to my prayer, which is not from deceitful lips.*

PSALM 17:1 NASB

Have you ever thought much about motives? Certain people are masters of ulterior motives—they always seem to have an underlying reason for saying or doing something. What seems like an act of kindness may actually be an attempt to get their own way.

When you look at Psalm 17, it's obvious the psalmist didn't have ulterior motives. His purpose was just. He wasn't deceitful. He didn't request things from the Lord in a deceptive way. His word was his word. He supported good and right causes.

As he had a clear conscience, he could pray to the Lord with complete transparency. God knew the psalmist's prayer was just and worth His holy attention. God knew the psalmist was a truth teller. He could listen to his honest prayer. As you approach the Lord of lords, remember to come to Him in absolute truth. Live a just, honest life and you won't have to question the Lord's response to your prayers.

Lord, I want my motives to be completely pure before
You and others. You know all; I'd be a fool to try to hide
anything from You. Please listen to my honest prayers.

A Long Time

Now it was at this time that He went off to the mountain to pray, and He spent the whole night in prayer with God.

LUKE 6:12 NASB

Before Jesus chose His twelve disciples, He went off by Himself to pray on the mountain. This decision wasn't an easy one. For one thing, He would've known the way Judas Iscariot would one day betray Him. And because it was difficult to choose those in whom He should invest His life and teaching, He wrestled with the decision and sought His Father all night long.

As the Son of God, Jesus could model the ultimate example of how to pray. Accordingly, when you have a huge decision to make, don't be afraid to spend a lot of time in prayer. Wrestle with your thoughts and feelings before the Lord. Sometimes a quick prayer just won't be sufficient. Ponder while you pray. Ask for guidance and wisdom. Don't stop praying, but keep seeking the Lord's will.

Lord Jesus, thank You for being such an amazing example.
Thank You for showing Your followers how to persist in
prayer. I don't want to give up or get tired of praying.

Delight Yourself in the Almighty

"For then you will delight yourself in the Almighty and lift up your face to God. You will make your prayer to him, and he will hear you, and you will pay your vows."

JOB 22:26–27 ESV

What do you delight in? Think of something that brings you great delight. Do you get to enjoy it very often?

Have you ever given much thought to delighting yourself in the Almighty? As the Giver of all good gifts and Creator of all, He is the One who enables your delight. How often do you stop to contemplate and appreciate how very good He is? When you recognize His great love and lift up your face to Him and pray with delight, He will hear you. If you've vowed or promised Him anything, it's natural to fulfill those vows as you delight yourself in Him.

Almighty God, You truly are amazing! You could've chosen absolutely anyone in this world to know You. I'm so thankful You've chosen me! I stand in awe of You and delight myself in You!

Right versus Wrong

"For the eyes of the Lord are on the righteous and his ears are attentive to their prayer, but the face of the Lord is against those who do evil."

1 Peter 3:12 niv

Most people realize that good, right choices should result in rewards, or that bad, wrong choices should result in consequences. A lot of times those rewards and consequences seem like they're only experienced in the here and now.

Yet the Bible clearly talks about lasting, eternal rewards and consequences. If you choose to do evil, the face of the Lord is against you. That's a harsh condemnation. But if you choose righteous living, not only does the Lord keep His eyes on you, but His ears are attentive to your prayer. He listens to you. He is for you and not against you. The difference between His favor and His displeasure hinges on your personal decision to live righteously.

Oh Lord, I want You to hear my prayer! I want Your eyes to be on me in a favorable way. Please help me make right, righteous choices in my life!

Deliver My Soul!

Then I called on the name of the LORD:
"O LORD, I pray, deliver my soul!"

PSALM 116:4 ESV

Have you ever felt like you've been taken captive by something? It might be hard to break away from recurring thoughts or compulsions. As much as you try to resist doing or thinking something you know you don't want to do or think, you keep returning to the same pattern. You might feel shackled by a repetitive sin, or you might realize your obsession with a subject or thing or person has become an idol.

When you feel trapped, you can pray for the Lord to set you free. The psalmist knew he could call on the name of the Lord. And when he did pray, what did he ask? He cried, "O Lord, deliver my soul!" If you could use some deliverance in your life, try the same prayer!

Oh Lord, I pray, deliver my soul! You know
what has captivated me. You know what I
need to break free from. Please set me free!

Teach Us to Pray

It happened that while Jesus was praying in a certain place, when He had finished, one of His disciples said to Him, "Lord, teach us to pray, just as John also taught his disciples."

LUKE 11:1 NASB

Imagine if you had been one of Jesus' disciples. The Son of God, in the flesh, was your personal teacher and mentor. Not only did you see how He treated people and responded to situations, but you also heard exactly what He said. As one of the people closest to Him, you could literally ask Him anything.

Since Jesus' disciples knew how much He prayed, one day they asked Him to teach them to pray. What an excellent request. Jesus' disciples realized that if anyone on earth knew how to communicate with almighty God, He did. And since they already knew and loved Jesus, they knew He would openly teach them. If they were to be discipled by Him and take up His ways as their own, they needed to learn the way He prayed.

Lord Jesus, thank You for coming to earth. And thank
You for openly teaching Your disciples how to pray.

Praying to Your Father

"Father, hallowed be Your name. Your kingdom come."
LUKE 11:2 NASB

As Jesus began to teach His disciples how to pray, He started His prayer by addressing His Father. Praying to His Father placed His relationship first—He didn't pray to anyone else but His Father.

Not only did He start by naming the One to whom He prayed, but He also praised His heavenly Father by affirming that His name is hallowed. Holy. Set apart. Worthy of respect and reverence.

After beginning His prayer with adoration and praise, Jesus asked for His holy Father's kingdom—His hallowed rule and reign—to come. How could God's kingdom come to earth then? How could His kingdom come to earth today? And how will His kingdom come in the future? As you learn to pray to your heavenly Father like Jesus did, ask for His kingdom to come today. Ask to see how He could even accomplish this through you.

Father, Your name is holy. I praise You above all else.
Please bring Your kingdom here to earth. Please
use me to do some of Your kingdom work. Thank
You for the privilege I have to pray to You!

What You Need

"Give us each day our daily bread."
LUKE 11:3 NASB

When Jesus taught His disciples to pray, He began with the most important focus: God the Father. The Father's holiness and kingdom were honored.

After focusing on the Father, though, Jesus taught His disciples to bring requests to the Lord through prayer. His requests weren't over-the-top extravagant but were centered on necessities. And His requests didn't include long-range hopes and dreams. He simply asked for God to give us each day our daily bread.

As you learn to keep your focus on the present—instead of the past or the future—you'll be freed from unnecessary concerns. And when you pray about necessities, you'll begin to see God as your generous Provider rather than an impressive magician who seemingly pulls your whims and fantasies out of thin air. Today, try praying for your immediate necessities and see how your focus in prayer might change.

Father God, thank You for the gift of today. Thank
You that I can trust You for everything I need. Thank
You for providing a place for me to live and food to
eat. Thank You for the people You've placed in my life
today. I pray You'll give me just what I need today.

Praying for Forgiveness

"And forgive us our sins, for we ourselves also forgive everyone who is indebted to us. And do not lead us into temptation."

LUKE 11:4 NASB

As Jesus finished teaching His disciples how to pray, He included two topics absolutely everyone deals with but hates to address: forgiveness and temptation.

It's not easy to admit you're wrong and need to ask for forgiveness. And it's not easy to forgive other people when they've wronged you in some way. Yet forgiveness is essential in life and in prayer.

When you come to your heavenly Father in prayer, search your heart for ways you've sinned. Then tell Him you're sorry. If you're holding on to a grudge against someone else, release it through forgiveness. By both asking for and granting forgiveness, you'll clear your conscience and feel like a heavy weight has been lifted.

Once you've covered forgiveness, it's time to address a likely cause of your sin: temptation. Ask for the Lord to protect you from temptation so you won't be so quick to fall into sin. As you honestly pour out your heart before the Lord with repentance and a request to avoid temptation, you'll have a clear understanding of the Lord's forgiveness and protection.

Father, please forgive me! I've sinned against
You, and I'm so sorry. Please protect me from
the enticement and temptation of sin.

Peace through Prayer

Do not be anxious about anything, but in every situation, by prayer and petition, with thanksgiving, present your requests to God. And the peace of God, which transcends all understanding, will guard your hearts and your minds in Christ Jesus.

PHILIPPIANS 4:6–7 NIV

Peace seems so elusive when you're in the middle of worrying. You wish you could have it, but how? How do you experience peace? The secret is found in Philippians 4. Instead of choosing to become anxious, pray to God and present your requests to Him in every single situation.

When you feel worries start to well up inside of you, stop and pray. Tell God whatever concerns you. Bring Him your fears. Express your hopes and wishes. Ask Him anything.

When you do, you'll begin to experience the peace of God. You won't understand how He does it, but He'll quiet you with His love and fill you with His peace in a beautiful way.

> Father, thank You for Your peace! Even if I can't understand it, I'm so grateful for the way it calms my fears. Thank You for being so willing to listen as I bring all my concerns to You.

A Reminder

Answer me when I call, O God of my righteousness!
You have given me relief when I was in distress.
Be gracious to me and hear my prayer!

PSALM 4:1 ESV

How many times do you typically need a reminder? Do you have a good memory and remember most details? Or do you tend to be fairly forgetful? It's no surprise that the Lord is all-knowing. He doesn't need reminders, and He is never forgetful.

When you pray, bring to mind how the Lord has been faithful in the past. You can remind yourself of how He has come to your rescue. You can remember the amazing ways He has blessed you. As you do, you'll silence any doubts. Your life is filled with little and big reminders of the way the Lord has answered when you've called to Him. All of those answered prayers and blessings point to His graciousness and loving-kindness toward you.

God of my righteousness, thank You for answering me
when I call. Thank You for all the relief You've given me
when I've been in distress. Thank You for the many, many
ways You've proved Yourself faithful time after time.
May I always remember how good You've been to me.

Resisting Temptation

Now when He arrived at the place, He said to them,
"Pray that you do not come into temptation."

LUKE 22:40 NASB

Actress Mae West once quipped, "I generally avoid temptation unless I can't resist it." The fact of the matter is that temptation really is so hard to resist. There's something magnetic about forbidden fruit; once something is out of reach, it becomes so much more appealing.

Temptation has been around since Adam and Eve were in the Garden of Eden. In fact, temptation existed before sin.

As the only sinless man, Jesus knew the antidote to temptation: prayer. As He and His disciples arrived in the Garden of Gethsemane before He faced betrayal and crucifixion, Jesus tried to help prepare His disciples. He knew they'd face temptation, and He knew the one way to resist it was to pray. Like every single person since Adam and Eve, you'll face temptation today. Start praying now that the Lord will help you resist it.

Lord Jesus, You know how difficult it is to resist temptation.
Yet You were able to do it! Please help me stand strong.
Please help me avoid falling into temptation.

Hear and Forgive

*"Listen to the pleadings of Your servant and of Your people
Israel when they pray toward this place; hear from Your
dwelling place, from heaven; hear and forgive."*

2 CHRONICLES 6:21 NASB

When King Solomon dedicated the temple he built for the Lord, he gathered all of Israel together for the ceremony. Once the Israelites assembled, Solomon blessed them then knelt down, spread out his hands toward heaven, and praised the Lord in prayer. After his praise, he went on to ask the Lord to listen to the pleadings of His people when they prayed toward the temple. He asked the Lord not only to listen to the people's pleading, but to hear and forgive.

As you pray to the Lord and plead with Him, be sure to start by giving Him rightful praise. Once you've done that, you can humbly ask Him to hear your prayers and forgive your sins. In asking Him to hear and forgive, you're reminded of the awesome privilege it is to bring your prayers to the King of kings.

Lord God, there is no one like You. I worship You
and You alone! I praise You for the faithful and
kind way You keep Your covenant of love with Your
servants. Please hear from heaven and forgive me.

Asking for Prayer

Pray for us. We are sure that we have a clear conscience and desire to live honorably in every way.

HEBREWS 13:18 NIV

It might seem easy to pray for yourself. You know what you need to confess and how you need to repent. You're well aware of the requests and concerns you want to bring before the Lord. It's easy to pray for other people too. When you learn about specific prayer requests, you're willing to pray. But asking other people to pray for you? That can be difficult.

It's humbling to admit your weaknesses and struggles. Letting others into your mess can leave you feeling vulnerable. And unless you're in the habit of asking for specific prayers or feel particularly comfortable with someone else, sharing prayer requests might even seem like you're asking for a favor. But it's good to ask for prayer.

As members of the body of Christ, believers should pray for each other. When you're trying to glorify Christ by living honorably, it's good to have others praying for you. And it's good to pray for your sisters and brothers in Christ. As other believers pray for you, make sure to pray for them too.

Father, I'm so thankful I don't have to live my Christian life on my own. Please help me open up to other believers with my struggles and concerns so they can pray for me.

The Time to Pray

Therefore, let everyone who is godly pray
to You in a time when You may be found.

PSALM 32:6 NASB

Have you ever woken up in the middle of the night, only to find yourself tossing and turning and unable to fall back asleep? Have you used that time to pray?

Or have you ever felt an overwhelming desire to pray for someone or some situation in particular? Have you stopped to pray?

Sometimes the Holy Spirit leads you to pray at just the right moment. The timing might seem strange to you, but when you're feeling the nudge to pray, do it.

Similarly, when you feel called to seek the Lord, whether in prayer, in worship, or through the reading of His Word, do it. Right away. Don't wait. In those moments of nudging and urgency, the Lord is leading and guiding you. Those are the moments when He may be found. You don't want to wait and let the opportunity pass.

Lord God, thank You for quietly leading me. Please
help me pay attention to Your gentle promptings.
I want to pray to You when You may be found.

What's Your Ministry?

*"But we will devote ourselves to prayer
and to the ministry of the word."*

ACTS 6:4 ESV

In the early church, the twelve apostles realized they couldn't effectively both teach and minister to believers in practical ways. They realized they couldn't do all the work all by themselves. Wisely they began to divide the labor and appoint people to serve in effective ways. The believers chose seven men to focus on daily food distribution and waiting on tables. This extra help freed up the apostles to devote themselves to prayer and the ministry of the Word.

Like the early believers, you've been given a particular gift. You may be gifted in the ministry of the Word, or you may have a wonderful way of noticing the needs of others and serving in very practical but needed ways. Whatever your gift may be, devote yourself to prayer while you're serving, and watch how the Lord will bless your personal ministry.

Lord, thank You for the unique ways You've gifted
me. I pray You'll open up opportunities for me
to use my talents and abilities for Your glory.

Following Nehemiah's Example

"Lord, the God of heaven, the great and awesome God, who keeps his covenant of love with those who love him and keep his commandments, let your ear be attentive and your eyes open to hear the prayer your servant is praying before you day and night."

NEHEMIAH 1:5–6 NIV

While Nehemiah was living far from Jerusalem during the Israelites' exile in Babylon, he heard that the Jewish survivors were living in disgrace, Jerusalem's walls were broken, and the city gates were burned. Upon receiving this news, Nehemiah mourned for days. As he wept with grief and fasted, he also prayed.

In his prayer, he recognized and worshipped the Lord for who He is: the loving, covenant-keeping, great and awesome God of heaven. Once he addressed his prayer to the Lord, he asked for God to listen, see, and hear his prayer. On behalf of the Israelites, Nehemiah confessed their sins. Then he made his request.

Learning from Nehemiah, you can begin your prayers with a reverent recognition of who God is. You can humbly ask Him to listen to your prayer. Confess your sins and ask for forgiveness; then make your request. Praying this way serves as a good reminder of how awesome God is and how humbly you should ask for forgiveness and help.

Lord God of heaven, You are great and awesome.
Thank You for hearing the prayers of Your servants.

Praying for Restoration

For we are glad when we are weak and you are
strong. Your restoration is what we pray for.

2 CORINTHIANS 13:9 ESV

Think about some of the most meaningful and special relationships in your life. Naturally you think about those loved ones quite often. And most likely you would sacrifice a lot for these treasured people.

The apostle Paul had similar feelings for the Corinthian believers. He prayed for them to do what was right. He prayed for their restoration. And he rejoiced when they were proven strong.

Like Paul, keep praying for the treasured people in your life. Pray that they would come to know and love Jesus. Pray that they would choose to do what is right. Pray for them to be restored if they've experienced any brokenness. Pray for them to find strength not in themselves, but in the Lord.

Father, thank You for blessing me with some very special
people. I'm so thankful for them. I pray they'll worship
You in spirit and in truth. I pray You'll strengthen them
and bring restoration when they face difficulties.

Not From around Here

"Hear my prayer, LORD, listen to my cry for help;
do not be deaf to my weeping. I dwell with you
as a foreigner, a stranger, as all my ancestors were."

PSALM 39:12 NIV

Have you been feeling out of place in this world? For followers of Christ, this feeling, while really uncomfortable at times, is completely normal.

The fact of the matter is, you feel out of place because you are out of place in this world. You're not meant to be here forever. This world shouldn't feel like home.

For now, you're here as an ambassador of Christ—His representative in this lost, lonely, and confusing world. You're a foreigner here and a stranger. You may feel out of place, but you're not alone. The Lord is with you. He'll always hear your prayer. He'll listen to your cry for help. He'll never be deaf to your weeping. Call out to Him, and you won't feel so alone.

Lord, as much as I feel out of place and all alone,
You never leave me. You're always there, always
understanding. I may not be part of this world, but
I'm waiting to feel completely at home with You!

Prayer as Worship

There was also a prophet, Anna, the daughter of Penuel, of the tribe of Asher. She was very old; she had lived with her husband seven years after her marriage, and then was a widow until she was eighty-four. She never left the temple but worshiped night and day, fasting and praying.

LUKE 2:36–37 NIV

In certain life situations, it's easy to start to feel like you might not matter or you don't have much to offer. Perhaps a certain diagnosis leaves you feeling like you can't contribute much, or your marital status makes you feel like you've been labeled.

In the New Testament, Anna was a faithful, loyal prophet. Even though she was very old and a widow, she didn't let her age or singleness deter her. Every day she stayed in the temple to worship the Lord. She was known for fasting and praying both night and day.

For Anna, her devout prayers were an act of worship to the Lord Jehovah. As with Anna, no matter where you might find yourself in life, your prayers and fasting can be a continual act of worship to the Lord.

> Lord Jehovah, I am so thankful I can pray to
> You anytime and anyplace. I want to worship
> You through prayer for all my days.

When Prayers Aren't Heard

*"So as for you, do not pray for this people, nor lift up
a cry or prayer for them; for I will not listen when
they call to Me because of their disaster."*

JEREMIAH 11:14 NASB

When, in Psalm 32:6, the psalmist advised praying to the Lord while He may be found, it was good counsel, because the Lord may not always be found. The prophet Jeremiah realized this truth when he needed to deliver a message from the Lord to Judah—and it wasn't good news.

God chastised His people in Jeremiah 11:10 (NIV), saying, "Both Israel and Judah have broken the covenant I made with their ancestors." Because of that broken covenant, the Lord vowed to bring an inescapable disaster on them and not listen to their cries. He even went so far as to tell Jeremiah not to pray for them.

Unrepentant sin and broken promises to the Lord result in severe consequences. In fact, if you turn away from the Lord often enough, out of judgment He may refuse to hear your prayers. While He won't listen to those who turn away from Him, He will listen to the cries and prayers of those who obey and worship Him in holy fear.

Lord God, please forgive me of my sin! Please help me
realize how I've sinned against You so I might repent. Please
look on me with favor and compassion and kindness.

"Pray to the Lord for Me"

Then Simon answered, "Pray to the Lord for me so that nothing you have said may happen to me."

ACTS 8:24 NIV

If you know someone who is unaware of the Bible, biblical truth and characters and accounts might be completely foreign to that person. As a result, what might seem like an obvious sin to a longtime believer may be unknown to someone outside the church.

Back in the early church, Simon the sorcerer was a new believer who was fascinated by the Holy Spirit. In particular, Simon offered money to Peter and John if they would teach him how to give the gift of the Holy Spirit to others.

Peter's response—"May your money perish with you, because you thought you could buy the gift of God with money!" (Acts 8:20 NIV)—and his call to repentance stopped Simon in his tracks. Simon was quick to listen, and once he realized that what he had done was blasphemous, he asked Peter and John to pray to the Lord for him.

As you pray for others in your life, don't forget to pray for new believers. Pray for them to know and understand the truth, and pray for ways for you to come alongside them and help guide them as a sister in Christ.

Father, please use me in the lives of new believers.
Please help me point them to Your truth!

Praying to the God of Your Life

By day the LORD commands his steadfast love, and at night his song is with me, a prayer to the God of my life.

PSALM 42:8 ESV

Do you often ponder the ways God loves you? Each day, the Lord of heaven and earth fills your life with good things. He commands His steadfast, never-ending love in a way that blesses you. And at night, His song is with you like a comforting lullaby. All throughout the day and night, you're surrounded by His generous kindness, favor, and peace.

How can you even begin to thank God for all His goodness? Try praying. Pray to tell the Lord you notice the amazing ways He is working in your day. Pray to tell Him the many ways you love Him. Pray to ask Him how He might lead and instruct you. Pray to Him in a song of praise. Pray because He is the Lord of your life and you long to talk with Him.

Lord, thank You for commanding me and leading
me with Your great love. Knowing that Your song
is with me at night fills my heart with peace.

Praying for Helpers

Then he said to his disciples, "The harvest is plentiful, but the laborers are few; therefore pray earnestly to the Lord of the harvest to send out laborers into his harvest."

MATTHEW 9:37–38 ESV

Isn't it funny that in the old radio and television series *The Lone Ranger*, the Lone Ranger wasn't truly alone? He had his friend and partner, Tonto. Just as the not-so-Lone Ranger depended on his friend, there are no lone ranger Christians. You can't live on a mission to reach the world for Christ all by yourself. You can't expect to grow in your faith and maturity in a bubble. You need people.

Other people sharpen you, encourage you, challenge you, and help you grow. Jesus knew this truth—it may be one of the reasons He chose twelve disciples to pour His life into, or a reason He sent them off to minister in small groups.

Jesus knew many people needed to experience His truth and saving grace, yet these people needed to be introduced to Him. People—groups of believing people—needed to go out into the world as workers. When you're feeling like you're doing the Lord's work on your own, or that all His work is overwhelming, pray for helpers. Pray for the Lord to send other workers to labor alongside you.

Father, please call other workers to come and help plant
Your seeds and work for Your harvest. Please show
me where I can help, and send other helpers too!

Owning Up to Your Mistakes

Then all the people said to Samuel, "Pray to the LORD your
God for your servants, so that we do not die; for we have added
to all our sins this evil, by asking for ourselves a king."

1 SAMUEL 12:19 NASB

Time and time again the Israelites chose to disobey God's commands and side with their own human nature. Time and time again the Lord warned them about their disobedience, yet they continued to rebel. And time and time again the Israelites dealt with the consequences of their actions. When they begged the Lord for a king, Samuel, the prophet, priest, and judge, warned the Israelites about their rebellion. They asked Samuel to intervene on their behalf through prayer.

Finally they understood, confessed, and repented of their sin. Samuel encouraged them to serve the Lord with all their hearts. He admonished them to turn away from idols and turn toward the Lord. And he prayed for them.

Sometimes, if you're steeped in sin like the Israelites, you need to recognize how you've wronged God, confess, repent of your sin, and pray. You'd also be wise to ask someone else to pray for you.

Father, I have sinned against You and I'm so sorry. Please withhold Your righteous judgment from me. I want to turn away from my sin and serve You with my whole heart!

Don't Stop Praying!

And so, from the day we heard, we have not ceased to pray for
you, asking that you may be filled with the knowledge of his will
in all spiritual wisdom and understanding, so as to walk in a
manner worthy of the Lord, fully pleasing to him: bearing fruit
in every good work and increasing in the knowledge of God.

COLOSSIANS 1:9–10 ESV

When your prayers don't seem to be answered quickly, it's easy to get frustrated and want to give up. The apostle Paul specifically kept praying for his believing friends in Colossae though. As his prayers faithfully continued, he prayed for much more than good health or earthly blessings.

How did Paul pray? He prayed for his brothers and sisters in Christ to be filled with the knowledge of God's will in all spiritual wisdom and understanding. He prayed his friends would walk and live in a manner worthy of the Lord. He prayed these Colossian believers would be fully pleasing to their heavenly Father. He prayed they'd bear fruit in every good work. And he prayed they might increase their knowledge of God.

All these deep, spiritual requests were so much more than temporary, surfacy prayers. And all these requests were prayed without ceasing. How could Paul's unceasing prayers change the way you pray?

Lord God, please fill me with the knowledge of Your will in
all spiritual wisdom and understanding. I want to be fully
pleasing to You. Please help me bear fruit in every good
work. Please make my knowledge of You grow and grow.

Hearing and Listening

Hear my prayer, O God;
listen to the words of my mouth.

PSALM 54:2 NIV

Isn't it frustrating to realize no one has listened to a word you've said? You might share something that's been on your heart or a serious concern. Or maybe you're making a simple request. When you get absolutely no response or even a simple acknowledgment that you've been heard, you can start to feel pretty upset.

Sometimes when you're praying, you might wonder if God is really listening. Is He attentive to your prayer? Is He tuned in to your words? Even if He doesn't offer an audible response, He does hear. In fact, He hears every single one of your prayers. And He does listen to the words of your mouth. God will never tune you out or ignore what you say. He hears. He listens. And He loves and cares for you.

Father God, thank You for hearing me. Thank You for
listening to what I have to say. I'm grateful You pay
attention to every single one of my prayers. I'd love
to pray to You even more often than I already do.

Pray for Forgiveness

"Repent, therefore, of this wickedness of yours, and pray to the Lord that, if possible, the intent of your heart may be forgiven you."

ACTS 8:22 ESV

Once you come to realize the Lord knows all things, it's futile to try to cover up your sin. You know what you think and say and do, and He knows what you think and say and do.

Instead of putting on a big act and pretending you're holier than you really are, it's best to own up to your mistakes. Admit your struggles and confess your sins. Ask Him for help, earnestly repent, and work to turn around any problem behaviors, thoughts, or practices.

As you repent of your sin and pray that God would forgive the intent of your heart, your prayer will come before His throne of grace. Repent; then thank Him for His forgiveness, mercy, and grace.

Heavenly Father, I confess that I've sinned against
You and I'm so very sorry. Please forgive me for the
way I've cherished my own sin over my love for You.
Please help me turn from my wicked ways. I want
to live a pure and blameless life before You.

Listen to My Plea!

"And listen to the plea of Your servant and of Your people Israel, when they pray toward this place; hear in heaven Your dwelling place; hear and forgive!"

1 Kings 8:30 nasb

When King Solomon and the elders of Israel took the ark of the covenant up to the Lord's temple in Jerusalem, they also brought sacrifices and prayers to the Lord. Solomon knew that the Lord's temple was a sacred, holy place. He knew the Israelites were set apart and incredibly privileged to worship the God of the universe there. His prayers and pleas reflected the wisdom he had gained from serving the Lord.

Solomon humbly asked the Lord to hear the Israelites' prayers from His earthly temple. And he asked God to forgive their sins.

You may not need to travel to the Lord's temple to pray to Him today, but you can still plead for Him to listen to your prayers. You can humbly ask Him to hear you and forgive.

Lord God, I worship You as Maker of heaven and earth.
You are the Beginning and the End. In You, all things
hold together. I pray that You would hear my prayers and
forgive me for the ways I've sinned against You. You are
holy, and I long to worship You in Your dwelling place.

Making Things Holy

*For everything created by God is good, and nothing
is to be rejected if it is received with thanksgiving,
for it is made holy by the word of God and prayer.*

1 TIMOTHY 4:4–5 ESV

In the Old Testament, we can read long lists of rules dictating what the Israelites could and couldn't do. Certain things were viewed as clean, while others were unclean. Everything changed, however, once Jesus came as the fulfillment of the law. Grace entered the picture and replaced legalism. Suddenly, what had once been viewed as unclean could now be considered clean.

This shift in perspective wasn't easy for new believers who were used to the lawful way of living. The apostle Paul wanted to reassure these believers that all things created by God are good. In his letter to Timothy, Paul wrote that everything—clean and unclean—could be received thankfully. All things created by God can be made holy by the Word of God and prayer. Prayer has the power to change things, and it has the power to make things holy.

God, everything You've created is good! I pray I won't
unnecessarily reject things but rather look to You to
transform the unclean into clean and the profane into holy.

Wherever You Are

*Hear my cry, God; give Your attention to my prayer. From
the end of the earth I call to You when my heart is faint;
lead me to the rock that is higher than I. For You have been
a refuge for me, a tower of strength against the enemy.*

PSALM 61:1–3 NASB

Where is home for you? And where is the farthest you've ever been
from home? However far from home you've been, you've never been
too far away from the Lord. From the ends of the earth you can call
to the Lord and He'll hear your cry and pay attention to your prayer.

Whenever you feel weary in the middle of your journey—whether
it's an actual, physical journey or a challenging season of life—you can
call to Him. He'll lead you. He'll guide you. He can be your Safe Place
and your Strength. Wherever you find yourself, when you turn to the
Lord, He'll lead you in His truth. He'll become your Rock of strength
and your Fortress and Shelter in treacherous times.

Lord God, it's such a relief to know You're always
there. No matter where I find myself on this earth,
I can always pray to You. You are my Refuge and
my Strength. You are my Protection in times of
trouble. I put my trust completely in You.

The Forgiveness Factor

*"And whenever you stand praying, forgive, if you have
anything against anyone, so that your Father who is
in heaven will also forgive you for your offenses."*

MARK 11:25 NASB

When you've been wronged by someone, forgiveness isn't exactly the first thought that comes to mind. You may enjoy holding a grudge and rehashing all the wrong things that were said or done.

Forgiving someone who intentionally hurt you might seem unthinkable and repulsive. If you hold on to all your hurts, though, and keep a record of who has wronged you, not only will it eat away at your peace of mind, but it also will affect your relationship with the Lord.

But forgiveness will bring freedom. When you choose to forgive others, the Lord will forgive you. Just as you haven't lived a perfect life and are in desperate need of forgiveness, others need to be forgiven by you. Who do you need to forgive today?

Oh Lord, You know how much I need Your forgiveness. Yet
if I hold on to grudges and refuse to forgive people who
have hurt me, You know my unforgiving heart. Even though
it can be painful and humbling, please help me forgive.
And please lavish me with Your undeserved forgiveness.

"Please Pray for Me!"

Yet King Zedekiah sent Jehucal the son of Shelemiah, and the priest Zephaniah the son of Maaseiah, to Jeremiah the prophet, saying, "Please pray to the LORD our God in our behalf."

JEREMIAH 37:3 NASB

If you've looked into Israel's history, you know that for years they were caught in a sin cycle: they wandered from the Lord and cherished sin. God warned them, then judged and punished them for their sins. The Israelites felt sorry for their sins, repented, and walked with the Lord again, until they fell back into sin and the cycle repeated.

King Zedekiah was one of Judah's kings who chose not to pay attention to the words of the Lord. Yet even though he didn't seek the Lord, he asked the prophet Jeremiah to pray on his behalf.

Sometimes in life, you'll notice the ungodly around you and see that even though they refuse to seek the Lord, these same staunch unbelievers may ask you to pray for them. In times of trouble, even the ungodly recognize who the godly are. If you're known for your faith in Christ, you might find someone unlikely asking you to pray on their behalf.

Father God, I want to be known for my faith in You!
Even if the ungodly oppose You and me, I want to stand
strong. Please help me be approachable enough for
people to come to me and ask me to pray for them.

"Please Pray for Us!"

Brothers and sisters, pray for us.
1 THESSALONIANS 5:25 NIV

In the closing words of his letter to the Thessalonian believers, the apostle Paul gave simple instructions: "Pray for us." Paul knew that he and his fellow Gospel workers needed prayer. Whatever ministry the Lord brought their way needed to be covered in prayer. Their words, their decisions, and their actions all needed prayer.

Similarly, whatever you do needs prayer. Don't be bashful in asking others to pray for you and your daily walk with the Lord. And don't forget to pray for your brothers and sisters in Christ too.

When you know that someone is laboring for the Lord, pray. Pray for motives that honor the Lord. Pray for words and actions that exalt Him and not people. Pray for unity in the church. And pray for the Lord to move and guide in a powerful way. Don't stop praying!

Lord, I am so thankful for the way that prayers matter.
Sometimes the best thing I can do to help my brothers
and sisters in Christ is to pray sincerely. Please bring to
mind those who need my prayers today. Please intervene
in their lives and prosper their work for the Gospel.

For What Are You Known?

Now there was a man in Caesarea named Cornelius, a centurion of what was called the Italian cohort, a devout man and one who feared God with all his household, and made many charitable contributions to the Jewish people and prayed to God continually.

ACTS 10:1–2 NASB

The Bible includes account after account of people—both likely and unlikely—who followed and feared the Lord. One of these people was the centurion Cornelius. Even though he was part of the Italian cohort in Caesarea, he still was a devout believer. Not only was he known to fear the Lord, but he also helped the Jews financially. And he was known for his continual prayer.

In life, it doesn't matter where you live or what your job is. It doesn't matter if you come from a long line of believers or if you're the first in your family tree to fear the Lord. What does matter is what you believe and how you're letting your belief shape your life.

If you do fear the Lord, are you a devout believer? Have you shared your faith so that your entire household also worships the one true God? Do you financially support the church? And are you known for a lifestyle of prayer? If so, keep on doing what you so faithfully do. And if not, it's never too late to make some changes and start living a life fully devoted to your heavenly Father.

Father, I want my entire life to
show my love and devotion to You.

Keep Praying and Giving

Cornelius answered: "Three days ago I was in my house praying at this hour, at three in the afternoon. Suddenly a man in shining clothes stood before me and said, 'Cornelius, God has heard your prayer and remembered your gifts to the poor. Send to Joppa for Simon who is called Peter. He is a guest in the home of Simon the tanner, who lives by the sea.' So I sent for you immediately, and it was good of you to come. Now we are all here in the presence of God to listen to everything the Lord has commanded you to tell us."

ACTS 10:30–33 NIV

Cornelius was a devout man who feared the Lord and prayed continually. One day the Lord answered his prayers in a surprising way: an angel came to him with a message.

Once the angel departed, Cornelius jumped into action and did everything the Lord requested. He sent messengers to get Simon Peter from the home of Simon the tanner. And once Simon Peter arrived, Cornelius explained what happened and waited patiently for the message from Simon Peter.

The Lord may not send an angel to speak with you, but as with Cornelius, He hears your prayers and remembers your gifts to the poor. Keep praying and giving!

Lord, thank You for hearing my prayers.
I pray I'll do whatever You command me to do.

Holy Fire

As soon as Solomon finished his prayer, fire came down
from heaven and consumed the burnt offering and the
sacrifices, and the glory of the LORD filled the temple.

2 CHRONICLES 7:1 ESV

While King David wanted to build a house for the Lord, God told David that he wouldn't. David was a warrior king, and the Lord wanted a man of rest and peace to build His temple—David's unborn son, Solomon. Even before Solomon was born, the Lord said he would give peace and quiet to Israel all of Solomon's days and he would be the man to build the Lord's house.

When Solomon finally did complete the temple and dedicate it with prayer, the Lord responded. He sent fire from heaven to consume the burnt offerings. The glory of the Lord filled the temple. The Lord had a specific purpose for Solomon, and Solomon knew it. When he completed the Lord's work and prayed, God answered.

Just as the Lord listened to Solomon's prayer and took action, He'll listen to your prayer. And while you may not experience holy fire coming from heaven, He'll respond to you as well.

Lord God, I stand in awe of You and Your majesty.
You are holy, yet You listen to my prayers. Thank You!
I worship You and want to do Your will for my life.

Have You Asked?

You do not have because you do not ask God. When you ask, you do not receive, because you ask with wrong motives, that you may spend what you get on your pleasures.

JAMES 4:2–3 NIV

So often it's easy to fool yourself into believing you can handle everything. You think if you can just work a little harder or try something different, everything will work out fine. But what if it's not all about you? Have you stopped to ask God first? Have you sought His help or guidance or ideas?

In his New Testament letter, James warns about checking your motives before you ask God. The Lord knows your heart and your motives; there's no fooling Him.

When you know you have good intentions and good motives, don't be shy. Ask your heavenly Father! If your motives aren't as honorable as you'd like, you may need to reexamine your heart. Or you may just need to keep asking, all the while seeking the Lord. In the process, you might notice something different about your motives, or your prayers might change completely.

Father God, I don't want to be shy with my requests.
But I also want to ask with pure motives. Please
help me show discernment in my requests!

Praise for Answered Prayer

Praise awaits you, our God, in Zion; to you our vows will be fulfilled. You who answer prayer, to you all people will come.

PSALM 65:1–2 NIV

When David praised God in Psalm 65, he knew a few things. First, he fully intended to fulfill his vows to the Lord.

Second, he knew that God answers prayer. In fact, David's life was filled with examples of times when he prayed and God faithfully answered. David knew for a fact that God answered with awesome and righteous deeds.

The third thing David knew is that all people would come to the Lord. He knew God would welcome all who call upon Him, both Jew and Gentile. Birth didn't matter; a person's heart did. God knows who truly seeks Him and will answer those prayers. Accordingly, He can and should be praised!

Father God, I praise You! You are so very good to me. Thank You for answering my prayers. I am so grateful I can come to You just as I am.

Keep Praying!

So Peter was kept in the prison, but prayer for him
was being made to God intensely by the church.

ACTS 12:5 NASB

Not every follower of Christ experiences an easy, problem-free life. In fact, many times the opposite is true. But if hardships can be expected, believers have one powerful line of defense to help brothers and sisters going through trials: we can pray.

When the apostle Peter was imprisoned for his faith, the early church didn't just walk away and forget about him. They prayed intensely for him.

As a result of their prayers, an angel of the Lord visited Peter in prison, loosed his chains, and led him out of the prison so that he left there untouched. What a miracle! Peter's friends were astonished to see him alive and free.

Just as their fervent prayers made a difference in Peter's life, your prayers can make a difference in the lives of other believers as well. Keep praying for the sisters and brothers in your life who face trials!

Lord God, I'm grateful prayer makes a difference.
Please help Your followers boldly speak the truth,
knowing that You can and will act in amazing ways.

Secret Prayers

"And when you pray, you must not be like the hypocrites. For they love to stand and pray in the synagogues and at the street corners, that they may be seen by others. Truly, I say to you, they have received their reward. But when you pray, go into your room and shut the door and pray to your Father who is in secret. And your Father who sees in secret will reward you."

MATTHEW 6:5–6 ESV

When Jesus taught His followers how to pray, He said something that would've shocked the crowd: He specified not to pray like a hypocrite. So how did a hypocrite pray? They'd stand and pray in public, whether at a worship service or on a street corner.

Public prayer wasn't necessarily wrong, but the motive in praying was. They wanted to pray in public to be seen by others.

Jesus taught a different way of praying: praying in secret. He encouraged followers to hide away and pray secretly to the Father. Why in secret? Because God the Father is in secret and sees in secret. Jesus taught that private prayer would be rewarded not by passersby but by our heavenly Father.

Father, I can hardly wait to sneak away to pray to You.
Our private prayer times are a secret I treasure.

Keep It Short and Simple

"And when you pray, do not keep on babbling like pagans, for they think they will be heard because of their many words. Do not be like them, for your Father knows what you need before you ask him."

MATTHEW 6:7–8 NIV

After Jesus told His followers to pray in secret, He busted another myth about praying, showing that the eloquence and length of prayers are not what give prayer power.

Instead of babbling on and on with an abundance of words, Jesus encouraged people to keep their prayers to the point. Don't prattle on endlessly. Don't use the same businesslike, mechanical-sounding prayers over and over. Just pray! Keep in mind, your heavenly Father already knows what you need. And while He wants to hear what you have to say, He doesn't need excessive descriptions or explanations with flowery words. Keep your prayers simple instead of over the top. Say what you mean and leave it at that.

Father, it's a relief to know I don't need to try to
impress You with a bunch of words or certain
phrases. You know what's on my heart and mind.
You know what I need. May my words be few.

Pray in This Way

"Pray, then, in this way: 'Our Father,
who is in heaven, hallowed be Your name.' "

MATTHEW 6:9 NASB

In the New Testament, the fifth, sixth, and seventh chapters of Matthew detail Jesus' Sermon on the Mount. Speaking to a large crowd of His followers, Jesus taught many principles. After teaching them how not to pray, Jesus explained how they should pray, when they prayed in secret and got to the point.

Jesus' example of prayer started with a relationship status—He prayed to "our Father," not just His Father. Then He affirmed some facts about God the Father: He's in heaven, and His name is hallowed, or holy and set apart. After noting some praiseworthy facts about His Father, He was ready to continue to pray.

Likewise, when you pray, remember who listens to your prayers. Tell Him how and why you honor and treasure Him. Come before your heavenly Father in worship first.

Heavenly Father, You are holy and set
apart. I bow before You in worship.

Praying for God's Kingdom

*"Your kingdom come. Your will be done,
on earth as it is in heaven."*

MATTHEW 6:10 NASB

Once Jesus identified who He addressed in prayer—our Father—He asked for God's kingdom to come. He also asked for God's will to be done on earth. And He gave away a fact about heaven: in heaven, God's will is done. That truth may seem fairly obvious, but it sets heaven—God's kingdom—apart as a very different place than earth.

As you pray for God's kingdom to come here and now, you also can pray for God to use you as part of His kingdom work. And as you pray for His will to be done here on earth, use these words to remind yourself that sometimes—many times!—God's will is not your will. Regardless, you still can pray that His completely good, completely just, completely holy will is what will be done here on earth.

Heavenly Father, I can hardly wait to experience heaven.
What is Your kingdom like? How wonderful of an experience
is Your kingdom, where Your will is done continually? Please
give me patience and grace as I wait to worship You there.

Praying for Daily Needs

"Give us this day our daily bread."

MATTHEW 6:11 NASB

As Jesus taught His followers how to pray, He highlighted the importance of a relationship as He prayed to His Father. Filled with worship, He prayed for God's kingdom and will to be done. Then He made a request: that God would give our daily bread.

Notice that Jesus made a request for all believers. He didn't ask for long-term future needs. And He didn't ask for anything extravagant. He asked for bread. For today.

With His prayer, you can remember that God gives you what you need today. You don't have to worry about what He'll do next week or three months from now. Focus on today. And focus on what you really, truly need today.

As you humbly ask your heavenly Father to provide all you need today, you'll develop a healthy, accurate perspective on life.

Father, thank You for providing everything I need! You are so generous to give me even things I want. And thank You for the gift of today. I don't want to take it for granted.

Asking for and Granting Forgiveness

"And forgive us our debts, as we also have forgiven our debtors."
MATTHEW 6:12 NASB

In Jesus' example of prayer, He worshipped the Father, prayed for God's will, and asked for basic needs for the day. Then He asked for forgiveness.

As a perfect, sinless man, Jesus didn't sin, but He knew His followers had plenty to confess. Once they confessed whatever people held against them, they could repent of their wrongs, ask for forgiveness, and move on.

After they asked for forgiveness, the next step was to forgive others. Forgiveness can be difficult to request and even more difficult to give. But Jesus made it a normal, necessary part of prayer.

Just as Jesus made forgiveness an essential part of His prayer, follow His lead! As you think over what you've been doing or thinking, what do you need to confess? And who do you need to forgive?

Heavenly Father, please forgive me of my sins. I've wronged people in this world, and I've wronged You. I'm so sorry. Please help me to let go of grudges and bitterness. Please help me forgive people who have sinned against me.

Prayers for Protection

"And do not lead us into temptation, but deliver us from evil."
MATTHEW 6:13 NASB

Jesus wrapped up His model prayer with two modest, humble pleas: Do not lead us into temptation. Deliver us from evil. Since Jesus was fully God and fully man, He experienced temptation yet always stood up against it. He knew that His heavenly Father could deliver Him from evil.

You and the Lord know your weaknesses. You know when and how it's easy to give in to temptation. Instead of caving to sin, you can pray for the Lord to keep you from temptation and guide you through enemy territory. He'll answer your prayer and provide a way out. You also can ask Him to deliver you from evil. Seek His protection, and watch for the ways He's at work.

Father, please protect me! I don't want to sin. Please
help me steer clear of temptation. And please deliver
me from evil too. Guide and guard my steps, please.

No Matter What

Praise be to God, who has not rejected my
prayer or withheld his love from me!

PSALM 66:20 NIV

When you examine your thoughts and your life, it can be easy to magnify your flaws. You might struggle with appreciating certain aspects of yourself or find it all too easy to focus on your weaknesses.

When you look at yourself critically, it's easy to wonder if the Lord should reject your prayer or if He might withhold His love from you. Yet He doesn't reject your prayer. In fact, He accepts it and listens attentively. And He doesn't withhold His love. He hears all your prayers and chooses to love you no matter what. With a God so attentive and loving, you should praise Him as soon as you think of it!

I praise You, Lord, because You are God. Thank You
for not rejecting my prayers. Thank You for showering
me with Your love and not withholding it!

One Special Baptism

Now when all the people were baptized, Jesus also was baptized, and while He was praying, heaven was opened, and the Holy Spirit descended upon Him in bodily form like a dove, and a voice came from heaven: "You are My beloved Son, in You I am well pleased."

LUKE 3:21–22 NASB

When Jesus prayed, miraculous events happened. He was known for healing the sick and driving out demons. But when He prayed while being baptized, the Father and Holy Spirit took part too. Heaven opened and the Spirit descended onto Jesus in an actual, physical form. Can you imagine?

God the Father also spoke audibly from heaven to affirm Jesus—not only did He specify that Jesus was His beloved Son, but He also said how pleased He was.

While the Father and Spirit could have been a part of other prayers that Jesus prayed, this instance is the only one recorded in scripture. It certainly set the scene for one very special baptism. And it certainly was an awesome response to prayer.

Lord, there is so much I don't understand about You.
But I worship You as my Lord and my God. Thank You
for the special roles of the Father, Son, and Spirit.

The Urgency to Turn from Sin

*"You have wrapped yourself with anger and pursued
us, killing without pity; you have wrapped yourself
with a cloud so that no prayer can pass through."*

LAMENTATIONS 3:43–44 ESV

The book of Lamentations is, not so surprisingly, a lament of all the devastation that obliterated the splendor of Israel. The Lord poured out His wrath and, like an enemy, multiplied mourning through His destruction. How could a loving God do such a thing? How could He be so angry as to pursue and kill? How could the Israelites' prayers not even pass through to His ears?

Israel had sinned, and false prophets never exposed the sin. While the Lord had warned of the impending judgment and wrath, His plans were ignored.

Israel's errors can serve as a sober warning to all of God's followers: Seek Him while He may be found. Live with a reverent fear of the King of kings, and obey His commands. Turn from sin. When you do, according to Lamentations 3, His great love will protect you from being consumed. His compassion will never fail. The Lord is good to those who hope in Him.

Heavenly Father, I humbly bow before You. I
have sinned and I am truly sorry. Please forgive
the many ways I've turned away from You.
Please hear my prayer and forgive my sins.

Devoted

Devote yourselves to prayer, being watchful and thankful.
COLOSSIANS 4:2 NIV

When you consider how often you pray, could you say that you're devoted to prayer? The apostle Paul gave his Colossian friends a good explanation of how they could devote themselves to prayer: by being watchful and thankful.

Just like the Colossians, you can be watchful throughout your day. What could you pray about? What events are happening that could use some prayer? Who does God bring across your path or into your mind? How can you pray for these things? Watch for any instance to pray, and then pray!

Similarly, what things are you thankful for each day? Did you watch a beautiful sunrise? Did a friend encourage you unexpectedly? Did you see God answer one of your prayers? Thank God for anything, whether it's little or big. As you thank Him for any and all things and watch for things to pray about, you'll find yourself more and more devoted to prayer.

> Father, what a gift to be able to come to You any
> time of the day or night and bring absolutely
> anything to You in prayer. Thank You for the
> privilege of prayer. I want to devote myself to it!

When Life Doesn't Make Sense

I call with all my heart; answer me, LORD, and I will obey your decrees. I call out to you; save me and I will keep your statutes. I rise before dawn and cry for help; I have put my hope in your word.

PSALM 119:145–147 NIV

Life doesn't always make sense. In fact, even now you might be walking through a time of confusion, when nothing seems clear or certain. In those times when you aren't sure what to decide, don't lean on your ever-changing emotions or what seems logical.

First, come to the Lord in prayer. Call to Him with all your heart. When you toss and turn thinking about life, get out of bed and cry for help. Read His Word so you understand what you're asked to obey, and then put your hope in what the Bible says. You can build your life on the truth of God's Word.

When God does answer you and offer direction, it's time to obey. Do what He asks you to do. As you call out to Him, put your hope in Him, listen, and obey, He'll give you the guidance and direction you need.

Father, I'm at a loss for words. I don't know what to do.
But I'm choosing to trust in You. Please help me!

Praying with Fasting

*When they had appointed elders for them in every
church, having prayed with fasting, they entrusted
them to the Lord in whom they had believed.*

ACTS 14:23 NASB

Throughout the Bible, praying with fasting is a popular and powerful combination. Fasting certainly is one tangible, practical way to humble yourself before the Lord. And while many of the Israelites fasted while mourning, early church leaders fasted and prayed during the process of appointing elders. After they'd fasted, prayed, and appointed elders, they entrusted the choice to the Lord.

You can use this same biblical example when you need to make an important decision. Paired with prayer, fasting can help you focus on seeking the Lord's direction. You can bring your petitions before Him, choose what seems to honor the Lord the most, then entrust your choice to Him.

Lord God, humbly I come to You for direction. Would
You please help me make the best choice? I believe
in You and trust You completely. I really want to
do Your will, whatever it may be. Please guide me
and make the best choice abundantly clear.

Praying When You Need It Most

Now when Daniel learned that the decree had been published,
he went home to his upstairs room where the windows opened
toward Jerusalem. Three times a day he got down on his knees
and prayed, giving thanks to his God, just as he had done before.

DANIEL 6:10 NIV

Daniel was in a seemingly difficult spot: obey the law or obey the Lord. Set as a trap for Daniel, the new law banned praying to anyone but King Darius. Yet without missing a beat, Daniel went home to the spot where he always prayed and continued to get down on his knees and pray to the Lord three times a day.

No matter the consequence, Daniel's faith was strong enough to withstand fear. Perhaps at no other time in his life did he need more prayer, so he prayed and prayed and prayed and asked the Lord for help. When the king's men discovered Daniel praying, they sent him to the lions' den. The Lord protected Daniel from harm because Daniel trusted in his God.

When you're asked to compromise or turn away from your faith, pray and stand strong. Like Daniel, trust in your God and keep praying.

Lord God, when Your enemies try to set a snare
for me, please protect me. I never want to stop
praying to You. I trust You completely!

Praying for Others Always

To this end also we pray for you always, that our God will consider you worthy of your calling, and fulfill every desire for goodness and the work of faith with power, so that the name of our Lord Jesus will be glorified in you, and you in Him, in accordance with the grace of our God and the Lord Jesus Christ.

2 THESSALONIANS 1:11–12 NASB

Have you ever wished that you had the apostle Paul as a personal friend? From all his New Testament letters, we can see that he had a heartfelt concern and love for other believers. As he confessed to the Thessalonian believers, he prayed for them always.

And what did he pray? He prayed that God would consider the Thessalonians worthy of their calling. He prayed the Lord would fulfill every desire for goodness. He prayed God would fulfill the work of faith with power.

And why did Paul pray for these specific requests? So the name of our Lord Jesus would be glorified in the Thessalonians. Those are some special prayers for special friends.

In your life, which friends are you led to pray for always? Pray for your friends to be considered worthy of their calling. Pray that the Lord will fulfill every desire for goodness and the work of faith with power. Pray for the Lord Jesus to be glorified in your friends' lives. Those powerful prayers will make an eternal difference.

Lord Jesus, thank You for the gift of friendships! And thank You that I can intercede in prayer on behalf of my friends.

In Trouble?

I cried to the LORD in my trouble, and He answered me.

PSALM 120:1 NASB

When you're in trouble, it's easy to feel alienated and alone. It might seem like the whole world is against you. It might feel impossible to find someone to trust.

In these moments of frustration, fear, and heartache, know you're not truly alone. Even though you don't see Him, the Lord is with you. You may not audibly hear Him, but the Lord will answer you. Cry out to Him. Tell Him your worries and fears. Bring all your thoughts and concerns to Him in prayer.

As you do, He'll answer you. You might watch situations line up in miraculous ways. People may surprise you in the way they're used by God to answer your prayers. You might hear a specific message in a book, sermon, song, or conversation that's a direct answer to something you've been praying about. However the Lord chooses to answer you, He will. Keep crying out to Him.

Lord, being able to turn to You when I need You most
is a huge relief. Even when it feels like everything else
is giving way, You stand strong. Even when I'm terrified
or in trouble, I don't have to run away. I can run straight
toward You with all my concerns. Thank You!

Prayers for Healing

*It happened that the father of Publius lay sick with
fever and dysentery. And Paul visited him and prayed,
and putting his hands on him, healed him.*

ACTS 28:8 ESV

Healing happened often in the New Testament church. Starting with Jesus, many sick people were healed and the dead were brought back to life. After Jesus rose from the dead and ascended into heaven, His disciples also began healing the sick.

The apostle Paul was another believer who could heal others. In the case of Publius's father, Paul's approach to healing involved praying and placing his hands on the sick man. That act of faith worked wonders, and the sick man's fever and dysentery were healed.

Prayers said in faith are powerful. In fact, they contain the power to do the miraculous.

Father, I know You have the power to heal. I
know You often heal here on earth but also might
hold off until You provide complete healing in
heaven. Please help me trust You in faith.

Everyone Is Welcome

*"Even those I will bring to My holy mountain, and make
them joyful in My house of prayer. Their burnt offerings
and their sacrifices will be acceptable on My altar; for My
house will be called a house of prayer for all the peoples."*

ISAIAH 56:7 NASB

When the Lord spoke to the prophet Isaiah, He revealed His plans for
Israel and foreigners. Isaiah 56 details how people from all the nations
would have access to the Lord. Anyone who loved the name of the
Lord and chose to bind themselves to Him would be welcome to serve
and minister to Him. Anyone who chose to hold fast to His covenant
and keep His Sabbath would find joy in His house of prayer. In fact,
the Lord's house would be called a house of prayer for all the peoples.

The Lord was ready and willing to gather all who loved and obeyed
Him. He was ready to accept the sacrifices of both Jew and Gentile.
He's ready to accept you, regardless of your heritage or upbringing.
Do you love His name? Do you choose to bind yourself to the Lord
God Almighty? Will you serve Him, minister to Him, and come to
His house of prayer?

> Lord, thank You for opening Your house of prayer
> to anyone who loves You. Thank You for including
> anyone who chooses to serve and hold fast to You!

Faithful in Prayer

Rejoice in hope, be patient in tribulation, be constant in prayer.
ROMANS 12:12 ESV

When the apostle Paul wrote to believers living in Rome, he clearly explained the truth and also gave plenty of sound instruction. After he encouraged believers to love others sincerely, he left simple instructions: Hate what's evil. Cling to what's good. Be devoted to each other in love. Honor others above yourself. Keep your spiritual fervor. Serve the Lord. Rejoice in hope. Be patient in affliction. Be faithful and constant in prayer. Share with believers who are in need. Practice hospitality. Bless people who persecute you. Live in harmony with others. Be humble.

Tucked in among all those imperative commands, you can find a powerful secret: be constant in prayer. Many of these directives seem humanly difficult. Bless people who persecute you instead of curse them? Live in harmony with hostile or rude people who disagree with you? Honor other people more than you honor yourself? Yet the impossible can be possible through prayer.

Be constant in prayer, and watch it transform your attitude and life.

Lord, I confess I selfishly want a lot of things that don't honor other people or You. Please help me faithfully pray about everything, and change my heart and mind through these prayers. Deep down I want to honor You most of all.

Seek Him

I cried out to God for help; I cried out to God to hear me.
When I was in distress, I sought the Lord; at night I stretched
out untiring hands, and I would not be comforted.

PSALM 77:1–2 NIV

When you've heard something upsetting, it can be difficult to think of anything else. The nagging thoughts lodge into your subconscious in a way that will wake you up in the middle of the night. If you're upset enough, you'll mull things over when you wake up and then throughout the day until you try to fall asleep at night.

When you're really troubled, it feels impossible to be comforted. Everyone experiences this at some point, and the psalmist Asaph put words to these feelings. In his distress, Asaph cried out to the Lord to hear him. He sought the Lord for help. When he couldn't sleep, he stretched out untiring hands.

Like Asaph, you can and should cry out to God when you're upset. Tell Him everything that's bothering you. Unload all your worries. When you're tossing and turning at night, pray. When your heart is so upset you feel no comfort, pray. Keep seeking the Lord in your distress. Keep praying in your darkest moments.

Oh Lord, please help me! When life is upsetting—
whether because of difficult people or circumstances or
a diagnosis—I'm filled with heart-wrenching emotions
of sadness and anger and regret. Rescue me, I pray!

Praying for Decisions

And they prayed and said, "You, Lord, who know the hearts of all, show which one of these two you have chosen to take the place in this ministry and apostleship from which Judas turned aside to go to his own place."

ACTS 1:24–25 ESV

Jesus' disciples had an important charge: being Christ's witnesses throughout all the earth. They knew they couldn't do it on their own. They also knew they wanted to keep twelve disciples and replace the position Judas Iscariot previously held. Jesus had carefully chosen them to be His disciples. How could they choose someone else to join them? After narrowing the field to two men who also had followed Jesus, the disciples needed to decide.

How did they make their choice? They prayed. They acknowledged that God knows the hearts of all, and they asked Him to show which one disciple He had chosen as a replacement. Then they cast lots. Those lots fell to one man: Matthias.

While decisions in your life may not seem quite as intense as choosing a twelfth disciple, you still face important decisions often. How do you make a choice? Like the disciples, acknowledge that the Lord knows the hearts of all. Ask Him to show you which decision is His will. Pray for a clear answer, and watch for His response.

You, Lord, know the hearts of all. Please show
me which path You have chosen for my life.
Please clearly guide my decisions!

Praying for Friends

*After Job had prayed for his friends, the LORD restored his
fortunes and gave him twice as much as he had before.*

JOB 42:10 NIV

When you're facing many problems and it feels like people you love
and trust are against you, read the book of Job. You might find comfort
and solace in the way Job faced his trials—and in the final outcome.

After all that his friends said—and they said quite a lot—Job prayed
for them. Job serves as an excellent example of someone who prayed
for his friends no matter what. While Job's friends did come to comfort
him for days, their empathy turned to blame.

Friends' intentions may change. What starts off as a good intention
can turn into something hurtful. While you can't control what your
friends say or do, you can control your response. Job didn't tear his
friends apart for their mean words. He prayed for them.

If and when your friends hurt you, either intentionally or unintentionally, choose to pray for them. You could pray for your response
and feelings to change, you could pray for your friends to realize how
they've made you feel, or you could pray specifically for the requests
and needs you know your friends have.

Father, thank You for the blessing of friends. Please
help me remember that my friends are people, and
sometimes people say or do hurtful things. Thanks
for the times they're helpful and encouraging.
Please help me be a good, supportive friend.

129

Praying Alone

*Then Jesus went with his disciples to a place called Gethsemane,
and he said to them, "Sit here while I go over there and pray."*

MATTHEW 26:36 NIV

The evening before He was betrayed, Jesus spent hours serving and pouring into His disciples at the Last Supper. He prayed for His disciples and future believers. Then, after the Passover meal, after Judas already left to betray Him, Jesus went to Gethsemane with the disciples. Jesus left His group so He could pray alone to His heavenly Father; He asked them to sit while He went off to pray. This was nothing new; Jesus often went off alone to pray.

If Jesus, the Son of God, needed to get away by Himself to pray, how much more do you need to do so? When you know you're at the cusp of facing difficulty, try slipping away from others to spend time praying alone. The quiet time with your heavenly Father will do wonders for your soul.

Lord Jesus, thank You for giving me so many examples
of how to live. Since You went away from people
to pray alone, I want to make it a priority too.

Surrendering Your Will

And He went a little beyond them, and fell on His face and prayed, saying, "My Father, if it is possible, let this cup pass from Me; yet not as I will, but as You will."

MATTHEW 26:39 NASB

One sign of maturity in a believer is found in a surrendered will. It's easy to think of what you'd like to have happen, but leaving things up to the Lord and truly welcoming His will in your life? That's not typically something a new believer will willingly accept.

As Christ spent the hours before His betrayal in prayer in the Garden of Gethsemane, He wrestled with the reality of what would come. He prayed His own will—that He wouldn't need to face what shortly would happen. Yet He included an important phrase: "yet not as I will, but as You will." As much as He didn't want to experience the cross, He was willing to do it if it was the Father's will for Him.

You may face an insurmountable challenge you really wish you didn't have to endure. Yet instead of grieving or wishing it away, may you find the courage to pray, "Yet not as I will, but as You will."

Lord Jesus, through Your life on this earth You taught me so much about life and love and how to honor God the Father. I pray I will have courage like You. I really do want the Father's will in my life and not my own.

Watching and Praying

"Watch and pray that you may not enter into temptation.
The spirit indeed is willing, but the flesh is weak."

MATTHEW 26:41 ESV

As Jesus labored in prayer in the Garden of Gethsemane, His disciples joined Him at a distance. Jesus, fully knowing what would happen, encouraged His disciples to do something to stand up against temptation: watch and pray. He recognized the human tendency to want to do the right thing but physically fail.

When you know the right thing to do, pray that you'll be able to follow through and do the Lord's will. Then watch out. Stay on guard against temptation, because it certainly will appear as a trap and a danger. As you watch and pray, you'll identify your temptations. Through prayer, you'll also strengthen your faith and resolve so that your flesh won't be so susceptible to stumbling.

Lord Jesus, You know the exact tendencies of humans.
As much as I may think I'm unique, I fall into the
same traps as others. Please help me watch out for
temptation and fight against it with prayer.

His Will

*He went away a second time and prayed, "My Father,
if it is not possible for this cup to be taken away
unless I drink it, may your will be done."*

MATTHEW 26:42 NIV

In His final hours on earth, Jesus knew what He would face. The weight of reality pressed down as He prayed in the Garden of Gethsemane. When He first prayed to His Father, He asked for another option—yet in an act of complete surrender, He added, "Yet not as I will, but as You will" (Matthew 26:39 NASB).

After asking His disciples to watch and pray that they wouldn't enter into temptation, He prayed alone again. In this second time of prayer, Jesus came to God the Father with a similar request: "May Your will be done." He realized that His agony, death, and resurrection might have been God's final decision. And as much as He didn't want to face it—or, in His own words, He wondered if the cup could not be taken away unless He drank it—He was willing to do the will of God the Father.

As you face the challenges of life, don't be afraid to keep asking God the Father to remove your trial. But ultimately, boldly surrender your will to Him. May His will be done in your life.

> Father, I don't always want to go through the
> difficulties I face. I pray that Your will would
> be done, though, and not my own.

What Is Righteousness?

*When the righteous cry for help, the LORD hears
and delivers them out of all their troubles.*

PSALM 34:17 ESV

Does righteousness sound unattainable? Does it seem like a lofty biblical concept that can't be realized in this life?

If you look at the actual definition of righteousness, you'll see it's not such an impossibility. To be considered righteous, you live a just, lawful life. You're ethical and honorable in your causes, conduct, and character. You're made right with the Lord.

When you're made right and recognized as making right choices, the Lord hears your cries for help when you pray. He delivers you out of your troubles. God's benefits to the righteous can be excellent motivators to choose to live in a just, right way.

Father, I want You to hear my prayers, and I'd love
for You to deliver me. Please help me make right
choices in Your eyes and live a righteous life.

The Prayers of Many

*You also must help us by prayer, so that many will give thanks on
our behalf for the blessing granted us through the prayers of many.*

2 CORINTHIANS 1:11 ESV

Have you ever experienced the power of the prayers of many people? If
you've faced a monumental crisis or know someone else who has, you
may have found out that dozens upon dozens of people were praying.
The prayers of even one or two people are powerful. But the prayers
of many people? They fuel the Lord's blessings.

The Lord loves to bless His followers. And He loves the prayers of
His people. As a matter of fact, prayers and blessings are inseparable.
Note in Paul's second letter to the Corinthian believers that the way
they could help was by praying—not giving, not serving in a special
way, not using their spiritual gifts. Their prayers helped. And when
their prayers resulted in blessings, many would give thanks.

When you find yourself wondering what you can do to help others,
pray! While you can offer to help in a different way, make sure your
first line of attack is prayer.

> Lord God, I don't understand the mysteries of prayer, but
> I do understand prayer is powerful in Your sight. Please
> help me turn to You in prayer before I do anything else.

Fasting and Praying for Others

But I, when they were sick—I wore sackcloth; I afflicted myself
with fasting; I prayed with head bowed on my chest.

PSALM 35:13 ESV

King David treated his enemies in a completely different way than they treated him. They sought to capture him and end his life, yet he didn't seek revenge. Instead of fighting back and attacking when he had the opportunity, David prayed for his enemies. And when he found out they were sick, he didn't celebrate and take advantage of the chance to harm them. He actually fasted, prayed, and wore sackcloth.

At times, fasting and praying for others can seem sacrificial. But fasting and praying for people who seek your harm? Seeking the Lord for people who repay your good with evil? David could do this because he was a man after God's own heart. He sought the Lord and honored his heavenly Father with his words and his actions.

If you're seeking the Lord and want to glorify Him, it will come at a cost. The cost may be comfort or pride. You may need to do some uncomfortable things, like pray and mourn for your enemies. As you do, remember the Lord knows your heart and intention. And He's pleased when you glorify Him.

Father, it can be so hard to pray for my enemies and treat
them in a way that honors You. Even when it's difficult,
please help me obey You instead of following my feelings.

Know a New Believer?

*When they arrived, they prayed for the new believers
there that they might receive the Holy Spirit.*

ACTS 8:15 NIV

When Jesus' apostles led the early church, their preaching and teaching reached the hearts of many. As a result, new believers in Christ multiplied, but because of persecution against the church, many of these believers were scattered. These scattered believers shared the Good News of Christ, and more and more people became believers.

While the apostles couldn't nurture each young Christian, they could continue teaching. They also prayed. By trusting the Lord through prayer, the apostles knew the new converts could mature and thrive, even in the face of adversity. What was one of their main prayers? That the new believers would receive the Holy Spirit. The apostles knew the power of the Holy Spirit in a person's life.

Like the apostles of the early church, you can pray for any new believers you personally know. Pray that they would receive the Holy Spirit and that their faith would grow and mature.

Father, thank You that prayer changes things. Through
prayer, You change people's hearts and lives. Thanks
for Your power and willingness to transform people!

How Do You Pray?

Now as Solomon finished offering all this prayer and plea
to the Lord, he arose from before the altar of the Lord,
where he had knelt with hands outstretched toward heaven.

1 Kings 8:54 ESV

Since prayer involves communicating with the Lord, you may wonder how you should pray. Should you kneel? Should you bow your head and close your eyes? Should you pray out loud or silently to yourself?

The wonderful thing about prayer is that you can do it in any way and at any time. You can think a prayer, sing a prayer, speak a prayer, or shout a prayer. You can pray while you're lying down, or while you're walking down the street. You can pray in or out of church. You can pray while you're traveling or when you're sitting still.

When King Solomon brought the ark of the covenant into the temple of the Lord, he prayed an important, solemn prayer of dedication. And he prayed by kneeling down and stretching out his hands toward heaven.

When you know you have an extra-important prayer or a serious plea, you can follow Solomon's lead by kneeling down and stretching out your hands toward heaven. When you finish your prayer, rise up in confidence, knowing the Lord has heard you.

Father, You alone are worthy of all my
praise and adoration. You alone I worship.

Praying Big Prayers

And it is my prayer that your love may abound more and more, with knowledge and all discernment, so that you may approve what is excellent, and so be pure and blameless for the day of Christ, filled with the fruit of righteousness that comes through Jesus Christ, to the glory and praise of God.

PHILIPPIANS 1:9–11 ESV

In your prayer life, do you find it easy to get stuck in a rut of small prayers? Do you stick to safe subjects like thanking the Lord for your food or health or for keeping you safe? Do you bring to the Lord specific requests for friends and family members? Do you focus on temporal, tangible requests? Or do you trust God with big prayer requests?

The apostle Paul was known for praying big prayers for other believers. For his friends in Philippi, Paul prayed that their love would abound more and more with knowledge and discernment. He prayed that they would approve what's excellent, that they'd be pure and blameless, and that they'd be filled with the fruit of righteousness that comes through Christ.

Try praying a big prayer like that and watch how God begins to answer it!

Father, I pray that my own love will abound more and more, with knowledge and all discernment, so that I may approve what is excellent, and so be pure and blameless for the day of Christ, filled with the fruit of righteousness that comes through Jesus Christ, to Your glory and praise.

The Relational Key

I say to the LORD, "You are my God."
Hear, LORD, my cry for mercy.
PSALM 140:6 NIV

Relationship is everything in communication. Having close ties with someone else grants you a different kind of access.

Think of someone who has a close relationship with you. When they come to you to talk, you want to listen, right? When they call your name, you answer, and you love spending time together.

The same is true if you have a relationship with the Lord. When you say to Him, "You are my God," you can rest assured He loves spending time with you. He wants to listen to you, and He'll answer you. You can cry to Him for mercy and know that He hears you. Because of your relationship with Him, your prayers carry a special kind of significance.

Lord, You are my God! I'm so thankful for that, and so
thankful for the way You know and love me. Thank You
for listening to my prayers and my cries for mercy.

Something about Jesus

About eight days after these sayings, He took along Peter, John, and James, and went up on the mountain to pray. And while He was praying, the appearance of His face became different, and His clothing became white and gleaming.

LUKE 9:28–29 NASB

Through prayer, you have a direct connection with God the Father. When Jesus prayed, His connection was filled with glory. In fact, while Jesus was praying on a mountaintop with Peter, John, and James, they saw His face change and His clothing become gleaming white.

Normal humans don't start shining when they pray, but then again, Jesus was no ordinary human. While He prayed on this mountaintop, Moses and Elijah came to talk with Him, and God the Father audibly spoke His approval: "This is My Son, My Chosen One; listen to Him!" (Luke 9:35 NASB). Again, that's something that doesn't normally happen to mere humans.

Even if your prayers don't get the same response as Jesus' prayers, God still listens to you. You're not His Son or His Chosen One like Jesus was. But when you pray and choose to worship His Son, His Chosen One, He'll hear you.

Lord Jesus, I worship You! I can't imagine what You were like when You lived here on earth. But You were holy and completely righteous. Just as people worshipped You and left all they had when they met You, I worship You too!

He Has Heard Your Prayer

And the LORD said to him, "I have heard your prayer and
your plea, which you have made before me. I have consecrated
this house that you have built, by putting my name there
forever. My eyes and my heart will be there for all time."

1 KINGS 9:3 ESV

When King Solomon finished building the house of the Lord, the Lord appeared to him a second time. The Lord assured Solomon that He heard his prayer and his plea. The Lord consecrated His special house and planned to stay there for all time.

For Solomon, this message was extraordinary. The one true God came to tell him that the time and treasure he had invested into building the Lord's house were worth it. The Lord would make His home there.

You may not build a special house for the Lord, but when you look around your life, you can see other building projects. You're continually constructing your relationships with your loved ones and creating connections with new friends, as well as building on the spiritual foundation in the place you call home. As you build into these worthy investments, don't forget to pray about them! The Lord will hear your prayer and your plea. And He just may set apart the house you build.

Father, I pray You'll look kindly upon the work of my
hands and the work of my heart. Will You please set apart
my home and my relationships for Your good work?

Thanking and Praising

I will give to the LORD the thanks due to his righteousness,
and I will sing praise to the name of the LORD, the Most High.
PSALM 7:17 ESV

Appreciation is a pretty good thing. When you do something for someone else, whether giving of your time or energy or giving a gift, knowing the recipient appreciates what you've done can feel especially gratifying. Sometimes a simple thank-you is all it takes to make you feel valued. But when no one seems to notice what you've done, it's easy to feel like your effort and thoughtfulness haven't been appreciated.

Just as you feel happy when people recognize what you do and offer thanks or praise for a job well done, the Lord appreciates thankfulness and praise too. And if you deserve thanks and praise for your earthly efforts, how much more does He deserve gratitude and adoration?

Stop for a moment and give thanks to the Lord. You could thank Him for all the wonderful things He has done for you, or you could thank Him for His righteousness. Once you've thanked Him, give praise to His name!

Lord, You are the Most High. I praise You for Your
righteousness. I thank You for all You've done
in my life and in Your creation. You are so very
good! You alone are worthy of my praise.

At an Acceptable Time

But as for me, my prayer is to you, O Lord. At an
acceptable time, O God, in the abundance of your
steadfast love answer me in your saving faithfulness.

PSALM 69:13 ESV

In today's society of instant gratification, waiting feels difficult. We want to see results right away or something feels wrong. Need hot food? Get it right now using a microwave or pick it up at a drive-through. Looking for an answer? Ask the internet. Want to watch a particular movie or show? Stream it instantly. Shopping for something specific? Get it delivered to your door within a day.

An instant sort of life isn't normal though. And God is not an instant sort of God. The Lord works and acts and answers prayers at an acceptable time. That time isn't necessarily acceptable to you. It's His acceptable time. It's His perfect timing and His perfect way. It probably won't be the timing you expect or hope for, but in His saving faithfulness the Lord will answer your prayers at His acceptable time.

Lord God, my prayer is to You. Even if it feels difficult,
I will wait for You to answer me at Your acceptable time.

144

The Strength to Escape

"But stay alert at all times, praying that you will have strength to escape all these things that are going to take place, and to stand before the Son of Man."

LUKE 21:36 NASB

God's Word never promises an easy, carefree life. In fact, the opposite is true. Trials and troubles are guaranteed. For believers in Christ, opposition should be expected.

Jesus taught us how to face challenges though: stay alert and pray for strength to escape tribulation and stand before Him.

As you stay alert at all times, you'll recognize what's happening in the world, especially as the day of the Lord gets closer. If you read the Bible and pray for the Holy Spirit to guide you, you'll notice what in this world you need to avoid or question. You'll understand what does and doesn't glorify God.

Once you're staying alert, pray and keep on praying. Pray for strength for both you and your loved ones. Pray that you'll escape the catastrophes and panic and persecution. Pray that you'll have strengthened faith and be able to stand before the Son of Man.

Father, please help me! Please help me stay alert as
Your day draws nearer and nearer. And fill me with
Your strength, I pray. Help me escape the danger that
is already happening and will happen in the future. As
long as I have breath, I want to stand strong for You!

Where to Go? What to Do?

Then all the army officers, including Johanan son of Kareah and Jezaniah son of Hoshaiah, and all the people from the least to the greatest approached Jeremiah the prophet and said to him, "Please hear our petition and pray to the Lord your God for this entire remnant. For as you now see, though we were once many, now only a few are left. Pray that the Lord your God will tell us where we should go and what we should do."

JEREMIAH 42:1–3 NIV

When the prophet Jeremiah stood up for the truth of the Lord, people noticed. Not only did they know that the Lord spoke through him, but they also knew Jeremiah prayed powerfully.

To make sure God heard their own prayers, "all the people from the least to the greatest" as well as all the army officers asked Jeremiah to pray for them. And what was their prayer request? "That the Lord your God will tell us where we should go and what we should do."

You can learn a lot from this request. For one, you can pray for the Lord your God to tell you where you should go and what you should do. Moreover, if you need help and direction, don't be afraid to ask godly people to pray for you.

Lord God, I'm looking to You for direction and guidance!
Thank You for listening to my prayers and answering them.
Please tell me where I should go and what I should do.

Pray When You're Asked

"I have heard you," replied Jeremiah the prophet. "I will certainly pray to the LORD your God as you have requested; I will tell you everything the LORD says and will keep nothing back from you."

JEREMIAH 42:4 NIV

Once the exiles of Jerusalem and Judah asked the prophet Jeremiah to pray specifically for the Lord to tell them where to go and what to do, Jeremiah did. After all, when people come to you asking you to pray to the Lord your God, how can you refuse?

Jeremiah certainly prayed and told the Lord the remnant's request. He also promised not to hold back anything—once the Lord responded to Jeremiah, he would relay the entire message.

Like Jeremiah, you'll never know when people may come to you with a prayer request. You may know their beliefs and spiritual state, or their background may be a bit of a mystery to you. Count it an honor that they esteem you and your faith in God. And be encouraged that they're open to praying to the Lord. They may even be convinced of God's power, mercy, and love. When someone asks you to prayfor them, count it all joy and pray right away!

Lord God, You are worthy of our prayers. You listen
and You answer. I want to be faithful in prayer.

Take Up Your Weapon

*Take the helmet of salvation and the sword of the Spirit, which
is the word of God. And pray in the Spirit on all occasions
with all kinds of prayers and requests. With this in mind, be
alert and always keep on praying for all the Lord's people.*

EPHESIANS 6:17–18 NIV

When you think of prayer, do you think of it as an effective way to engage in battle? As the apostle Paul describes spiritual armor in Ephesians 6, prayer helps you defend yourself and you can take up the helmet of salvation to protect yourself. As you pray, you can take up the sword of the Spirit. With that sword, the Word of God, you'll both learn the truth that defends you and then use it to attack the enemy. Nothing defeats lies quicker than the truth.

As theologian John Piper says, "Prayer is the power that wields the weapons of warfare. . . . Prayer is not a civilian device."* When you're in the middle of a spiritual or physical battle, pray. When you feel Satan's arrows targeting you, pray. Grab the Word of God and arm yourself. Fight back against his heinous lies with God's glorious truth. And do it all backed by much prayer.

Father God, thank You for equipping me with spiritual
weapons. With prayer providing the power, please help both
my salvation and Your Word to protect and defend me.

*John Piper, "Prayer: The Power That Wields the Weapon," *Mission Frontiers*, June–July 1989, www.missionfrontiers.org/issue/article/prayer-the-power-that-wields-the-weapon.

Let Your Words Be Few

Guard your steps as you go to the house of God, and approach to listen rather than to offer the sacrifice of fools; for they do not know that they are doing evil. Do not be quick with your mouth or impulsive in thought to bring up a matter in the presence of God. For God is in heaven and you are on the earth; therefore let your words be few.

ECCLESIASTES 5:1–2 NASB

Prayer is your opportunity to tell the Lord about anything that's on your mind. While it's good to be comfortable with Him—He does know your every thought, after all—it's also good to remember that He's the Lord of the universe. Instead of yammering on about every random thought that pops into your mind, be intentional in your prayers. And be reverent. As Ecclesiastes advises, let your words be few.

As you enter into the presence of the one true God, recognize that He is worthy of your worship, praise, and adoration. Guard yourself as you worship Him, and approach to listen rather than talk. As King Solomon knew very well, it's proper to use discernment in prayer. Don't be quick with your mouth or impulsive in your thoughts. Think before you speak, and think before you pray.

Father, I worship You as Lord of all.
I long to listen to You in worship.

Open Doors

And pray for us, too, that God may open a door
for our message, so that we may proclaim the
mystery of Christ, for which I am in chains.

COLOSSIANS 4:3 NIV

The apostle Paul devoted his life to the Gospel. Traveling from city to city, he proclaimed the Good News of Christ to the lost and taught believers wherever he went. Authorities weren't pleased with his message though, and Paul's travels ended as he was imprisoned. Yet living a life under arrest didn't stop his urgency to reach others for Christ. He implored believers in Colossae to pray for God to open a door for his message even while he was in chains. Even though he suffered for proclaiming the mystery of Christ, he prayed for an opportunity to continue.

You may never find yourself in prison because of Christ. But you still can pray for God to open a door for your message, so that you may proclaim the mystery of Christ. And remember to pray for your brothers and sisters in Christ who are proclaiming His Good News around the world!

Lord God, please open a door and give me a
spirit of boldness, so I can proclaim the mystery
of Christ to those who don't know You!

When You Call

I call upon the LORD, who is worthy to be praised,
and I am saved from my enemies.

PSALM 18:3 ESV

If you've ever been threatened by enemies, you know how terrified and powerless you can feel. It's easy to spiral into a thought pattern where you rehash what was said or done over and over. It's also easy to dwell on fearful possibilities. But life doesn't need to be like that, even if you're dealing with enemies.

When you call upon the Lord, you recognize that He is God. He's in control, and He has a master plan. He can and should be praised for all that He is and all He can do. Once you call on Him and praise Him, you can relax in your trust in Him. Since He has chosen you, He'll save you too—not only from your sins once you die, but from your enemies here on earth. All you need to do is call on Him.

Father God, I turn to You for help. You are great
and mighty, and I praise You! Please save me
from my enemies, both seen and unseen.

All Day Long

It is good to give thanks to the LORD, to sing praises to
your name, O Most High; to declare your steadfast love
in the morning, and your faithfulness by night.

PSALM 92:1–2 ESV

No matter what you might be facing today—great joy or great sorrow, unexpected pleasures or searing pain—it's good to give thanks to the Lord. In the middle of everyday life, it's good to sing praises to His name. When you give thanks and sing praise, you declare His steadfast, never-ending, never-changing love and faithfulness both to Him and to yourself. If you happen to thank and praise Him in front of other people, you'll affirm His great love and faithfulness to them as well.

If you begin to praise Him when you wake up every day, your daily focus will be set on Him, making it easier to declare His steadfast love in the morning. And when you fall asleep each night, try thanking Him for His faithfulness throughout your day and all the ways He worked in your life and in the people around you. By starting and ending your day thinking of the Most High and praising Him, you'll find that the entire focus of your perspective and life will change.

Lord, You are good! Your mercy endures forever. I praise
You because You are the Most High. Thank You for Your
never-ending love. Thank You for being a faithful God.

Praying for Daybreak

Fearing that we might run aground somewhere on the rocks,
they cast four anchors from the stern and prayed for daybreak.

ACTS 27:29 NASB

When you've suffered through a sleepless night, maybe one of the most difficult aspects is waiting for the sun to rise. If you could just see a glimmer of light, you'd know the long, dark night will finally be over. You could get up with a fresh start, even if you feel exhausted after a night of tossing, turning, and engaging in mental wrestling matches.

One time the apostle Paul sailed to Italy as a prisoner, and the ship he was traveling on ran into some severe storms. After being tossed by the wind for two weeks, the crew and passengers were certain their boat would sink. When they suspected they were close to land at nightfall, that night was filled with worries, but what did the passengers do? Cast anchors to stay in place and prayed for daybreak.

In the middle of a sleepless night, when worries leave you tossing and turning, pray for daybreak. The Lord just might break through your darkest night.

Father, in the middle of my darkest sleepless nights,
please help me see the light of day and the light of You.

The Prayer of the Upright

The LORD detests the sacrifice of the wicked,
but the prayer of the upright pleases him.

When you hear the word *upright*, what comes to mind? A piano? Sitting or standing straight and tall? Living an honorable, just, and moral life?

Proverbs talks about the prayers of the upright—the virtuous, righteous, and noble. And what about the prayers of these honorable individuals? They please the Lord.

Not everyone pleases the Lord. In fact, He detests the wicked. Their sacrifices are an abomination to Him. If He feels so strongly about their sacrifices, there's no way their prayers would please Him.

If you want the Lord to be pleased with your prayers—and who wouldn't?—attempt to live an upright life. Notice that *upright* doesn't mean perfect and flawless. Maintain honorable, noble intentions and make just, virtuous choices, and your prayers will be pleasing to the Lord.

Oh Lord, I long to be pleasing in Your sight!
Please help me make upright choices day by day.

Bow Down before Him

*Come, let us bow down in worship, let us kneel before
the LORD our Maker; for he is our God and we are the
people of his pasture, the flock under his care.*

PSALM 95:6–7 NIV

In the midst of your busy days in this chaotic world, do you take much time to kneel down and worship the Lord? Or is it all too easy to fall into the trap of thinking you can worship Him in the middle of your busyness?

While all things—from the most mundane chore to the most profound act of service—can be done as worship, how often do you pause to focus on the Lord? Regularly slowing down to read and ponder His Word is wonderful, and so is stopping to focus on prayer.

As you live a life of worship through the things you do, also make sure you worship through quiet times focused on your Maker and Shepherd. As you do, He'll lead you step by step in a clear direction. You'll learn so much more about Him and His tender personality as you allow Him to guide you with His loving care.

Lord God, You are my Maker and my tender Shepherd.
I want to take more time to worship You.

Prayers for Healing

"Return and say to Hezekiah the leader of My people, 'This is what the LORD, the God of your father David says: "I have heard your prayer, I have seen your tears; behold, I am going to heal you. On the third day you shall go up to the house of the LORD." ' "

2 KINGS 20:5 NASB

When the prophet Isaiah told King Hezekiah to set his house in order because he was going to die, King Hezekiah did what just about anyone would do: he prayed and wept profusely. There's nothing quite like getting an upsetting medical diagnosis to make you weep and turn to the Lord.

After his praying and mourning, the Lord chose to heal King Hezekiah. While not every sick, God-fearing person will be healed in this life, this account of Hezekiah's life shows that God listens to prayers.

The Lord sees your tears. He hears your prayers. And sometimes, in the midst of your deepest sorrows, He steps in and brings healing and restoration. If you're sick, you don't know if the Lord will choose to heal you or not. But especially in your uncertainty, don't give up praying for healing. Keep seeking the Lord and crying out to Him.

My Lord and my God, please remember how I have walked before You wholeheartedly and in truth, and have done what is good in Your sight! Please bring healing!

Help in the Middle of Distress

In my distress I called to the LORD; I cried to my
God for help. From his temple he heard my voice;
my cry came before him, into his ears.

PSALM 18:6 NIV

When you're in distress and feel like you're at the absolute end of your rope, it's obvious you're not in control of the situations you face. You feel like you can do nothing and have nothing to offer. In those moments, look up. Call to the Lord in your distress. Cry to Him for help and beg Him for mercy.

As the psalmist promised, in those moments when you're crying out and calling to God, He hears your voice from His temple. You're not too far for Him to hear you, and you're not too desperate for Him to help. You can place all your trust and hope in Him alone.

Lord God, please help me! In my darkest moments
when it feels like all hope is gone, I choose to trust in
You. I cling to You alone and beg You for mercy.

Boldness through Prayer

On the day I called, You answered me; You
made me bold with strength in my soul.

PSALM 138:3 NASB

You've probably heard the seemingly trite phrase "Prayer changes things." But the saying actually isn't trite, because it's profoundly true. When you come to the Lord through prayer and call out to Him, He'll answer. He might not change your circumstances or the things that are weighing you down, but He just might change you.

The Lord has the power to transform a soul. He can make the weak strong. He can make the cowardly bold. He can inspire the quiet with words of power and truth. He can calm an agitated spirit and bring peace to a worried mind. As you call to Him, He can give you a supernatural strength that will make you bold for Him. That boldness begins when you turn to the Lord Almighty in prayer.

Father, I feel so weak. Please give me strength! When I feel timid, please fill me with Your boldness. When I don't know how I'll take my next step, please empower me. I trust You!

In Jesus' Prayers

"I pray for them. I am not praying for the world, but for those
you have given me, for they are yours. . . . My prayer is not
for them alone. I pray also for those who will believe in me
through their message, that all of them may be one, Father,
just as you are in me and I am in you. May they also be in
us so that the world may believe that you have sent me."

JOHN 17:9, 20–21 NIV

After His Last Supper, Jesus encouraged His disciples, trying to prepare their hearts for what they'd face without Him; and He prayed. John records that Jesus prayed for Himself, for His disciples, and for future believers—that's you.

Jesus' main prayer for future believers was unity. He wanted believers to be one in the Lord. And what was the reason for this unity? So that the world may believe that God the Father sent Jesus.

You can become an answer to Jesus' prayer by making unity important. Instead of taking offense too easily or looking for ways to divide yourself from other believers, search for common threads that can keep you united. Cling to your common belief in Christ and celebrate it.

Thank You for thinking of me and praying for me in Your
final hours on earth, Jesus. Please help me choose unity
over division. Please unite me with other believers so the
world may believe You were sent by God the Father.

159

Standing in the Gap

Now when I heard these words, I sat down and wept and mourned for days; and I was fasting and praying before the God of heaven.

NEHEMIAH 1:4 NASB

Even though he was exiled from Jerusalem and living in Babylon, Nehemiah grieved when he heard about Jerusalem and the status of Jews who survived the captivity. In fact, Nehemiah wept, mourned, fasted, and prayed before the God of heaven for days. This wasn't just a quick little prayer for him. He grieved and petitioned the Lord for days.

In your life, you'll hear about people who endure horrific trials. You'll be taken aback when you consider certain challenges that people face. But your concern and sympathy shouldn't just end once you forget about the bad news. You can enter into the struggles of others. You can lift them up in prayer. You can weep and mourn. You can fast and pray. As you do this for others and with others, you'll be standing in the gap.

Lord God, when I know someone is facing something
dire or if I'm grieved by a particular situation,
please help me truly mourn, fast, and pray. Please
allow my sincere prayers to make a difference.

Acceptable

Let the words of my mouth and the meditation of my heart be
acceptable in your sight, O LORD, my rock and my redeemer.

PSALM 19:14 ESV

So often it's easy to get caught up in discerning what's acceptable. What's an acceptable outfit to wear to an event? What's an acceptable thing to say to someone you're just getting to know? What's an acceptable status update to post on social media? What's an acceptable way to behave in public?

When you care what others think, trying to figure out what's acceptable is a normal part of life. But how often do you stop to consider what's acceptable to the Lord?

In Psalm 19, David prays that the words of his mouth and the meditation of his heart would be acceptable in God's sight. Your choice of acceptable speech can range from your prayers to what you thoughtfully say to others to the words that come flying out of your mouth in a hasty response. Your choice of acceptable meditations involves those things that catch and hold your attention, as well as the topics you intentionally ponder. Are these words and thoughts acceptable to the Lord?

Father God, I want my speech and meditations to please
You. Please let them be acceptable in Your sight!

Pouring Out Your Heart

*Trust in him at all times, O people; pour out your
heart before him; God is a refuge for us.*

When you pour out your heart to someone, you typically confide in someone you know well and trust completely. There's always an element of risk, though, as there's always a chance your confidant could break your trust.

God is a confidant who never will betray your trust. You can trust Him completely and pour out your heart before Him, knowing He will hear you. You will be completely safe taking refuge in Him. As you pour out your heart, sharing all your hopes, fears, good news, and concerns, He can be trusted with your deepest secrets. And, unlike the people in whom you may confide, He has complete power to intervene.

Trust in the Lord at all times! Pour out your heart before Him. God is a Refuge for you.

Heavenly Father, even when it feels like I have no one on this earth to trust or confide in, I always have You. Thank You for being my Safe Hiding Place. Thank You for being my Refuge.

Prayer's Surprising Power

Now about midnight Paul and Silas were praying and singing hymns of praise to God, and the prisoners were listening to them; and suddenly there was a great earthquake, so that the foundations of the prison were shaken; and immediately all the doors were opened, and everyone's chains were unfastened.

ACTS 16:25–26 NASB

Beaten, thrown into jail, and locked in chains because they had disrupted the sinful ways of the citizens of Thyatira, Paul and Silas prayed and sang praises to God long into the night. The prisoners who happened to be in jail with them couldn't help but listen to all that Paul and Silas prayed and sang.

In the middle of their praying and praising, an earthquake rattled the prison's foundation, unfastened all chains, and opened the prison doors. While the Bible describes what happened to the jailer—he was saved and baptized, along with his entire household—we never find out what happened to the other prisoners who witnessed the miraculous. Were their lives forever changed by prayer?

If you feel locked in some sort of prison today—maybe a prison of your thoughts or habits or addictions—don't be afraid to pray and sing praises to the Lord. You never know when your shackles will fall away and your prison door will swing open!

Father, nothing can stop You from working. Please release me from my prison, and set me free in You!

Please Listen

"Now, my God, please, let Your eyes be open and Your
ears attentive to the prayer offered in this place."

2 Chronicles 6:40 NASB

Understanding exactly how the Lord had blessed him and the Israelites, King Solomon was serious about praying to the Lord. Especially when he built and consecrated the Lord's temple, he sought to honor and obey the Lord. During the temple's dedication, Solomon specifically asked the Lord to open His eyes and ears to the prayers offered in the temple. Instead of taking the Lord's attention for granted or just expecting Him to always see and hear, Solomon humbly asked.

Everyone can learn a lesson from wise King Solomon. Instead of taking prayer for granted or assuming God will listen to your prayer, truly be grateful to approach the Lord of heaven and earth. Instead of barging into His presence, praise Him for who He is and humbly present your requests. As you do, you'll remember that He is God and you're not.

Father God, I praise You for Your power and might. I
praise You for Your goodness and grace. Please let Your
eyes be open and Your ears attentive to my prayers.

The Lifter of My Head

But You, LORD, are a shield around me, my glory, and the One who lifts my head. I was crying out to the LORD with my voice, and He answered me from His holy mountain.

PSALM 3:3–4 NASB

When you feel burdened and weighed down by life's troubles, it's hard to imagine a way out. Problems appear magnified and seem to multiply. It can be so easy to focus on what's wrong. Yet your perspective doesn't need to be like that—even when you face challenges.

Even in troubling times, you can cry out to the Lord and choose to remember that He is your Protector. The Lord is your Shield. He's your glory and honor and renown. He lifts up your head so you don't have to focus your vision on what's below. And when you switch from looking down to looking up, your entire perspective changes. You'll see things in a different light when the Lord lifts your head and you focus on Him instead of your earthly concerns.

> Lord, You are my Shield! You are my glory! You answer me! And You lift my head so I don't need to focus on my troubles. I praise You!

Let Me Tell You

Come and hear, all you who fear God; let me tell you what he has done for me. I cried out to him with my mouth; his praise was on my tongue. If I had cherished sin in my heart, the Lord would not have listened; but God has surely listened and has heard my prayer.

PSALM 66:16–19 NIV

When something wonderful happens to you, it's natural to want to tell everyone the good news. In your excitement, you can't help but share. The same is true when you realize God has done something wonderful in your life.

The psalmist was very excited to share his good news with everyone who fears the Lord. And what did God do? He listened to the psalmist's prayer. The psalmist praised the Lord and cried out to Him. In response, God listened and heard his prayer.

The next time you realize the Lord has heard you and answered your prayer, tell someone! Don't be shy about giving God the glory and telling others all that He's doing in your life.

Lord God, thank You for listening to me. Thank You for hearing my prayer. And thank You for answering me. I want to tell those who fear You all about Your faithfulness!

Praying for Boldness

And when they had prayed, the place in which they were gathered together was shaken, and they were all filled with the Holy Spirit and continued to speak the word of God with boldness.

ACTS 4:31 ESV

God does big things when His people pray. He has ever since creation and He continues to answer prayers in amazing ways.

One major response to prayer happened when the early church began to grow. After Peter and John faced opposition from the Sadducees, chief priests, and elders, they returned to their companions and prayed. After their prayer, God moved in a big way: the place where they were meeting was physically shaken and the believers were filled with the Holy Spirit then spoke the Word of God with boldness.

As He did in the early church, God can move in you and through you too. He'll fill you with the Holy Spirit so you can speak the truth of God with boldness. In case you find yourself dealing with fear or uncertainty, pray for boldness. When you need to teach or speak the Word of God, pray for boldness. He'll be gracious to give it!

Lord God, I want to bring Your truth to others.
Please help me boldly speak Your Word!

Your Faithfulness

Then Hezekiah turned his face to the wall and prayed to the
Lord, and said, "Please, O Lord, remember how I have walked
before you in faithfulness and with a whole heart, and have
done what is good in your sight." And Hezekiah wept bitterly.

ISAIAH 38:2–3 ESV

After you've been walking with the Lord for a while, you begin to create a personal history of faith. You remember significant moments when you went out on a limb to trust the Lord and He protected or provided for you. You can recall specific prayers He has answered. You know how you've been changed by the different ways you've served Him. As you've loved Him, followed Him with all your heart, and chosen to avoid sin, you've added to your faith and faithfulness.

King Hezekiah was the same. He had quite a faith journey and story of faithfulness to the Lord, so when he was sick and the Lord told him to prepare to die, Hezekiah was heartbroken. Turning his face to the wall, he wept bitterly by himself and prayed. In his prayer, he asked the Lord to remember his history of faith. The Lord did and extended Hezekiah's life.

In your own prayers, don't be afraid to ask God anything. You never know how your life of faithfulness and faith will play into your requests.

Father, I want to walk before You faithfully with a
whole heart! I want to do what is good in Your sight.

When You're Thrown for a Loop

*I call on you, my God, for you will answer me; turn your
ear to me and hear my prayer. Show me the wonders
of your great love, you who save by your right hand
those who take refuge in you from their foes.*

PSALM 17:6–7 NIV

Life won't always unfold like you might expect—in fact, it rarely does.
So when you feel like you've been thrown for an unbelievable loop,
take a deep breath and call on the Lord.

When you're facing trouble and call on Him, don't be afraid to ask
Him for specifics. Humbly ask Him to listen to you. Ask Him to show
you the wonders of His great love. Ask Him to give you wisdom—
wisdom for what to say and what to do. Ask Him for help with every
challenge. Ask Him to save you from your foes. And ask Him to give
you peace. Then, once you've made your requests, step back and trust
the Lord. Give your worries to Him, and let Him work out His plan
in your life.

Lord God, please hear my prayer and show me the wonders
of Your great love for me. Thank You for saving me through
Christ. Please save me now from my foes here on earth.

Mercy!

Have mercy on me, my God, have mercy on me, for in you I take refuge. I will take refuge in the shadow of your wings until the disaster has passed. I cry out to God Most High, to God, who vindicates me. He sends from heaven and saves me, rebuking those who hotly pursue me—God sends forth his love and his faithfulness.

PSALM 57:1–3 NIV

Have you ever felt so completely overwhelmed by life and so out of control that you've given up and cried out for mercy? When you cry out for mercy, you beg for compassion. You admit you're subject to someone else's power and you need their favor.

While you may be in a certain situation where a person can grant you mercy, more often your problems are likely to stretch beyond human intervention. You need to beg God for mercy. He can protect you in the shadow of His wings. He can save you from pursuers. He can comfort you with His love and faithfulness.

Have mercy on me, my God, have mercy on me! I will take refuge in the shadow of Your wings until the disaster has passed.

Equipping Yourself through Prayer

"You did not choose me, but I chose you and appointed you so that you might go and bear fruit—fruit that will last—and so that whatever you ask in my name the Father will give you."

JOHN 15:16 NIV

Stop and think of the reality that Jesus chose you. Of all people, He appointed you. Why did He do this? For one, He chose you so you might go and bear lasting fruit. For another reason, He wanted the Father to give you whatever you ask in Jesus' name.

What kind of asking was Jesus talking about? Did He mean basic, everyday requests, or could there be something more?

Jesus taught this after He commanded His disciples to love one another as He had loved them. Jesus knew firsthand that loving people is messy and that it would be difficult for His disciples. But it is possible, especially with God the Father helping through answered prayers.

Teaching this right before He endured the cross, Jesus knew His followers would encounter resistance and suffering for His name. He knew their walks of faith would feel more like spiritual battlefields. He knew the only way they could be equipped to love when it seemed impossible was through prayer.

Just as the disciples could love against all odds because of the power of prayer, you can too.

Father God, please help me love others like Jesus did and does, even when it feels uncomfortable and difficult.

Complete Honesty

With my voice I cry out to the Lord; with my voice I
plead for mercy to the Lord. I pour out my complaint
before him; I tell my trouble before him.

PSALM 142:1–2 ESV

The Psalms provide a beautiful account of the way believers can pour out their hearts before God. Raw emotion doesn't need to be filtered when you're communicating with your Creator.

David, a man after God's own heart, definitely came to the Lord with all his emotions. Psalm 142 gives a glimpse of what he was feeling when he was on the run for his life. He cried out to the Lord, pleading for mercy. He poured out his complaints and told the Lord all his troubles. David didn't sugarcoat the truth of what he felt. He didn't try to think positively and make the best of the situation. He told God exactly what he felt, thought, and hoped would happen.

Be encouraged to come to God in the same way, especially when you face obstacles that seem insurmountable. When you're terrified or tired or hurt or reeling because someone has wronged you, tell your heavenly Father. When you share your whole self with Him with complete honesty, your relationship with Him will grow deeper and stronger.

Lord, I'm so thankful I can turn to
You and tell You exactly how I feel.

Before the Sun Rises

Very early in the morning, while it was still dark, Jesus got up, left the house and went off to a solitary place, where he prayed.

MARK 1:35 NIV

If you live in a full house, it can be very difficult to find a moment alone. Once a day gets started and everyone's up and moving around, life quickly becomes a buzz of activity, noise, and distractions. If you're a night owl, you could stay up once everyone goes to bed to pray, process your day, and spend time with the Lord. If you're an early bird, you can rise before anyone else to start your day with the Lord.

Time and time again, Jesus got up very early in the morning—before the sun rose—to get away to solitary places and pray by Himself. Disciples and crowds of people either couldn't or wouldn't distract or disturb Him when He was away alone.

Depending on your season of life, you may or may not have the opportunity to leave your house and go to a solitary place. But look for opportunities to get away and pray—maybe it's first thing in the morning before the sun rises, or maybe it's a spot where you can hide away and spend time in worship and prayer. Wherever and whenever it may be, start praying like Jesus did.

Lord Jesus, thank You for giving me an example of how and when to pray. Please help me find my own solitary place where I can meet with You in worship and prayer.

Obedience Is Key

"The LORD has said to you, O remnant of Judah, 'Do not go to Egypt.' Know for a certainty that I have warned you this day that you have gone astray at the cost of your lives. For you sent me to the LORD your God, saying, 'Pray for us to the LORD our God, and whatever the LORD our God says, declare to us and we will do it.'"

JEREMIAH 42:19–20 ESV

The prophet Jeremiah didn't mince words when it came to the remnant of Judah. Even though they asked Jeremiah to pray for them and claimed they would do whatever the Lord instructed, they chose to stray and disobey. That disobedience would end up causing judgment, famine, pestilence, and death by the sword.

Jeremiah's harsh words can serve as a warning to any God-fearing person. Keep your vows to the Lord. If you tell the Lord your God you'll do what He says, you need to do what He says. When you come to the Lord in prayer and He guides you, make sure you follow through in obedience.

My Lord God, please forgive me for the times when I've chosen to disobey You in defiance. Have mercy on me.

Exalt His Name

*I will bless the LORD at all times; His praise shall
continually be in my mouth. My soul will make its boast
in the LORD; the humble will hear it and rejoice. Exalt
the LORD with me, and let's exalt His name together.*

PSALM 34:1–3 NASB

Exalting the name of the Lord is a theme sprinkled through the book of Psalms. But what does it even mean? To exalt means to elevate, raise in rank or status, heighten, praise, glorify, and honor.

When you think of exalting the Lord in prayer, you can praise Him. You can boast about His goodness to you. You can lift up His name and give Him credit for all that He has done and is doing in your life.

Exalt the Lord's name in your own personal prayers, and exalt Him when you're around others too. Share His goodness and glory with the surrounding world so they can exalt His name with you.

I bless You, Lord God! My soul makes its boast solely in
You. You are high and lifted up, and I worship You.

Intercession

And the people came to Moses and said, "We have sinned, for we have spoken against the LORD and against you. Pray to the LORD, that he take away the serpents from us." So Moses prayed for the people.

NUMBERS 21:7 ESV

The Lord uses leaders to communicate with groups of people. Especially in the Old Testament, God used particular men and women to lead and guide His chosen people. Sometimes the leaders were prophets; sometimes they were priests. For the Israelites' exodus out of Egypt, the Lord used Moses.

Moses interceded on behalf of the Israelites many times. He met with the Lord on Mount Sinai and received the Ten Commandments. Often he acted as a middle man between the people and God.

Once when the Israelites complained to the Lord in frustration and impatience, fiery serpents were sent to bite and kill some of them. There's nothing quite like a fiery killer snake to grab your attention! When the Israelites realized they had brought this judgment on themselves because of their sin, they asked Moses to intercede through prayer. He prayed for them, and the Lord provided a way out. May your own prayers for forgiveness change God's judgment.

Father, please forgive me! Against You,
and You only, have I sinned.

A Community of Helpers

And they brought these men before the apostles; and
after praying, they laid their hands on them.

ACTS 6:6 NASB

In the early church, the disciples knew they couldn't accomplish all the work on their own. So they could focus on teaching and prayer, they needed to pass along responsibilities to other leaders who were devoted followers of Christ.

And how did the disciples decide on the servant leaders? They prayed for discernment. Then, after the leaders were chosen, the disciples prayed and laid their hands on them as a way to bless and commission them for their new roles.

If you serve the Lord, prayer is a vital part of your service. And if you're feeling overwhelmed by your responsibilities, it's time to pray for guidance and helpers. Keep prayer as a main part of your service; then watch the Lord multiply your time, energy, effectiveness, resources, and helpers.

Father God, I can't do everything on my own! I'm not meant to be alone in my walk with You either. You made me for a community of believers. Please show me where You'd like me to serve and who could possibly help me.

He Hears Your Prayer

*"Yet, Lord my God, give attention to your servant's prayer
and his plea for mercy. Hear the cry and the prayer that
your servant is praying in your presence. May your eyes
be open toward this temple day and night, this place of
which you said you would put your Name there. May you
hear the prayer your servant prays toward this place."*

2 Chronicles 6:19–20 niv

You can pray absolutely anywhere, yet there's something special about praying in a house of worship. Praying and worshipping where other believers gather is meaningful. And in the Old Testament, the temple was a particularly special place to pray.

When King Solomon dedicated the Lord's temple, he knew it was special. Solomon wanted the Lord to be present in and pleased with this holy place. Instead of just being hopeful, though, Solomon prayed to ask the Lord for His blessing. Specifically, he asked the Lord to open His eyes toward the temple at all hours of the day and night. And he asked the Lord to hear his prayer.

Just like Solomon, you can humbly come before the Lord and ask Him to open His eyes and ears as you pray, especially as you pray at church.

O Lord my God, I'm so grateful You pay attention
to my prayers. Please continue to open Your eyes
toward Your holy places. Please hear my prayer.

Everything Changes

"Because he has loved Me, I will save him; I will set him securely on high, because he has known My name. He will call upon Me, and I will answer him; I will be with him in trouble; I will rescue him and honor him. I will satisfy him with a long life, and show him My salvation."

PSALM 91:14–16 NASB

When you choose to love the Lord and trust in Him, everything changes. Rather than being punished as His enemy, you are saved as one of His chosen ones. Because you know His name, He will set you securely on high. When you call upon Him in prayer, He will answer you. He'll be with you in good times and in trouble. Instead of abandoning you, He'll rescue you. Instead of forsaking you, He'll give you honor.

All this blessing and favor in place of judgment and punishment comes as a result of love and trust. What do you choose today? Do you reject what God offers? Or do you choose to love the Lord and trust Him completely?

Lord God, what an enormous difference we can see in the lives of those who choose to love and trust You and those who choose to reject You. Thank You for giving Your blessings and favor to those who choose You.

In the Middle of a Crisis

LORD, you are the God who saves me; day and night I cry out to you. May my prayer come before you; turn your ear to my cry.

PSALM 88:1–2 NIV

When you're in the middle of a crisis, your reaction and attitude can shift unpredictably. One moment you might feel completely panicked, yet soon after you might swing to feeling angry or rebellious. And after you experience those strong feelings, you might feel like you just don't care. Then later on you're filled with hope and peace.

People of any age or stage can experience fluctuating emotions—adolescents aren't the only ones with mood swings. Yet whether you're experiencing a high or a low, you can always cry out to the Lord. He will listen to you at absolutely any time. He is the God who saves you and the One who turns His ear to your prayers. He sees what you're going through and wants to comfort you with His peace when you need it most.

Lord, I am so thankful You are the God who saves me! I'm so relieved I can call on You at absolutely any time. Thank You for hearing my prayers.

A Fond Farewell

When it was time to leave, we left and continued on our way. All of them, including wives and children, accompanied us out of the city, and there on the beach we knelt to pray. After saying goodbye to each other, we went aboard the ship, and they returned home.

ACTS 21:5–6 NIV

Sending someone off with a farewell can be so bittersweet. While you may be excited about a new adventure, it's also sad to say goodbye.

The apostle Paul was used to saying a lot of farewells as he traveled on his missionary journeys. When he left his friends in Tyre, prayer was a big part of his send-off. Entire families of husbands, wives, and children went with Paul and his fellow travelers out of the city and knelt on the beach to pray and say their goodbyes.

When you're saying goodbye to a loved one, stop to pray together. In addition to hugs, kisses, and waves goodbye, prayer can be a wonderful part of send-offs.

Father, thank You for the way You knit hearts together. Thank You for my dearest friends, family, and church family. When I do need to say goodbye, I want to pray intentionally with my brothers and sisters in Christ.

Near or Far

The LORD is far from the wicked, but He
hears the prayer of the righteous.

PROVERBS 15:29 NASB

When you know that someone doesn't like you and chooses to say and do pretty much everything you oppose, would you rather get nearer to them or keep your distance?

Even though Jesus taught to love your enemies and you strive to obey Him in this way, you might not seek out your enemies in order to give them a lot of your time and attention. Depending on how many people are clamoring for your attention, you likely spend most of your time focused on the people in your life who love you and want your influence.

If this is the case for you, you might be able to relate to the Lord in Proverbs 15:29. He's devoted to the righteous. He hears the prayers of those who please Him with their right choices and who seek after Him. The wicked though? The Lord is far from those who reject Him and do what is evil. Every day you have a choice—will you draw near to the Lord in righteousness, or will you stay far from Him in wickedness?

Lord, I want to make right, righteous choices that reflect
my love for You and my devotion to You. Please help me!

Facing Obstacles

Isaac prayed to the LORD on behalf of his wife,
because she was unable to have children; and the
LORD answered him, and his wife Rebekah conceived.

GENESIS 25:21 NASB

Since Adam and Eve ate the forbidden fruit in the Garden of Eden, every single person's life has been affected by the fall. Heartbreaking realities like death and infertility are part of everyday life.

In Genesis, when Isaac and Rebekah faced infertility, Isaac dealt with the obstacle the best way he knew: he prayed to the Lord. The Lord answered him, and Rebekah conceived twin sons.

When you face what seems like an insurmountable obstacle in your life—or you know someone else trying to make it through a struggle and crisis of faith—pray! Pray on your own behalf, or pray on behalf of someone you know. As you pray, watch for the ways the Lord answers your prayer.

Father, You never intended to have a world full of obstacles,
yet the fall has made them a normal part of life. I want
to bring all my troubles and trials to You in prayer!

Sounds of Silence

To you, LORD, I call; you are my Rock, do not turn a deaf
ear to me. For if you remain silent, I will be like those who
go down to the pit. Hear my cry for mercy as I call to you for
help, as I lift up my hands toward your Most Holy Place.

PSALM 28:1–2 NIV

When you're waiting for an answer or a response before you can move on or make plans, one of the most frustrating things to do is wait. There's not much you can do as you wait and wait only to hear silence.

King David knew this kind of frustration and asked the Lord to respond. He acknowledged the fact that God was his Rock and that he needed to hear from his Rock: "For if you remain silent, I will be like those who go down to the pit." Why did David need the Lord's response so very desperately? He was crying for mercy and calling to his heavenly Father for help.

When you're in need of mercy and help, silence can feel deafening. If you have an urgent need, cry out to the Lord in prayer. If nothing changes and you can't seem to sense Him responding, keep praying and asking for His response.

Lord, I'm trying to be patient, but I desperately
need Your help! Please listen to my prayer
and respond. I will wait for You.

Intense Prayers

And being in agony he prayed more earnestly; and his sweat became like great drops of blood falling down to the ground.

LUKE 22:44 ESV

Before Jesus was arrested and led to the cross to face His crucifixion, He knew what was coming. He spent the hours of dreadful anticipation in prayer. If anyone could remove Him from the situation, it would be His heavenly Father.

And if He needed to endure, only His heavenly Father could give Him the strength to face it all.

Jesus prayed and prayed in agony, even while His disciples slept nearby. He begged His Father to take this cup away from Him, and then He asked for His Father's will to be done. As He wrestled with what was to come, He prayed so fervently that His sweat fell to the ground like drops of blood. That's intense prayer.

When you're facing the most difficult challenges of your life, your prayers may become more intense than ever before. Keep praying, because that intensity and trust in the Lord will help carry you through your trials.

Father, I'm so thankful that in absolutely every situation I can come to You in prayer, even if I end up praying in agony.

Praying about the Sins of Others

*"So now, our God, listen to the prayer of Your servant
and to his pleas, and for Your sake, Lord, let Your
face shine on Your desolate sanctuary."*

DANIEL 9:17 NASB

If people choose to disobey the Lord and ignore His warnings, consequences follow. The Israelites experienced this reality during their Babylonian captivity. Daniel knew the Israelites had sinned, done wrong, acted wickedly, and rebelled. He also knew they received their deserved punishment. In Daniel's words, open shame belonged to them (Daniel 9:8).

Despite the sin of his people, Daniel knew he still could come to the Lord in prayer. He chose to plead with the Lord with fasting, sackcloth, and ashes. His request? That God would turn His anger and wrath away from the Israelites.

As a believer, recognize the importance of praying for your church and your nation. Intercede in prayer even if no one else does. Confess sins and ask for forgiveness. Pray for healing and changed hearts. Humbly ask the Lord to intervene—not based on your own merit, but because of His great compassion.

Lord God, I humbly come before You to beg You to
work a miracle in this country. Please draw hearts
to Yourself. Please open the eyes of the spiritually
blind, and turn people from their wicked ways.

Worthy of Your Praise

The LORD is great in Zion; he is exalted over all the peoples.
Let them praise your great and awesome name! Holy is he!

PSALM 99:2–3 ESV

Your prayers can and should be filled with praise. The Lord was great in Zion, and He is great in your neighborhood today. Even if it doesn't seem like He's at work in the people around you, He is! He's exalted, lifted up, and honored over all people.

Even if it seems like the world around you is filled with hopelessness, hope can be found in Him. Even when it seems like people exalt themselves, He will be the One exalted and praised. He is great, He is awesome, and He is holy.

As you remember all the amazing things our God truly is, praise Him! Tell Him what you appreciate about Him. Describe what you most respect about His character. Think about His qualities and what makes Him stand out above every single person. Then praise Him! He is great, and He is worthy of your praise.

Lord Jehovah, I stand in awe of You. You are amazing.
There is none like You in the entire universe.
I praise You for Your greatness and holiness.

Good Morning!

But I cry to you for help, LORD; in the
morning my prayer comes before you.
PSALM 88:13 NIV

On most mornings, what's the first thing that pops into your mind? Do you wake up to your alarm clock and hear the radio? Do you hear the noises from someone else in your home? Do you wake up thinking of all you need to do that day? Do you wake up with a start? Do you drift in and out of sleep until you decide it's finally time to roll out of bed? Or do you wake up praying?

One fantastic way to start your morning is by praising the Lord. Simply choose to do it, and then remind yourself when you wake up. You could set a reminder if needed. As soon as you remember, though, start your day by praising God for His awesome qualities. After you spend time thinking about His goodness, present some specific requests for your day. Then get up and get moving, knowing your entire day has been covered in prayer.

Father, in the morning when I rise, I want my first
thoughts to be about You. You are worthy of all
my praise. I love You and want to worship You!

Changed

Peter sent them all out of the room; then he got down on his knees and prayed. Turning toward the dead woman, he said, "Tabitha, get up." She opened her eyes, and seeing Peter she sat up.

ACTS 9:40 NIV

Have you ever studied the apostle Peter's life? A fisherman called by Jesus, Peter was bold and often spoke before he thought. Impetuously he did things like get out of a boat in the middle of a raging sea, cut off someone's ear, and propose to put up a shelter for Moses and Elijah during Jesus' transfiguration.

After he denied Christ three times, watched the crucifixion of his Lord and friend, examined the empty tomb, and talk with the resurrected Jesus, Peter was a changed man. He clearly spoke the Good News with authority and healed people. When Peter healed Tabitha, he got down on his knees, prayed, and told her to get up. That was all! And, in fact, Tabitha did get up.

You may or may not have a dramatic life transformation like Peter. You may never bring anyone back from the dead. But, like Peter, you can access great power through prayers of faith.

> Lord, thank You for the example of Peter! I love
> seeing how one normal man's life completely
> changed because of Jesus. Change me, please!
> And use my prayers in absolutely amazing ways.

Deep in Prayer

As she kept on praying to the Lord, Eli observed her mouth.
Hannah was praying in her heart, and her lips were moving but
her voice was not heard. Eli thought she was drunk and said to her,
"How long are you going to stay drunk? Put away your wine."

1 Samuel 1:12–14 niv

Sometimes when you concentrate deeply as you pray, you may forget your surroundings. You're talking with the God of the universe and pouring out your heart to Him. Maybe you're focusing completely on Him in praise. And as you fix your mind on Him, you might close your eyes and truly tune out the rest of the world.

In the Old Testament, a woman named Hannah dealt with the bitter sadness of infertility. One day, as she prayed about it at the house of the Lord, her prayers were so fervent and passionate that Eli the priest took notice of her. He mistook her for a drunken woman because of the way she moved her mouth in silence.

Imagine Hannah—so desperately heartbroken, so desperately pleading for the Lord to change her plight and bless her womb.

When you need to pray about whatever is vitally important to you, don't worry about how you might look to other people. Like Hannah, just pray!

Father God, I want to come before You in prayer at any
time and in front of anyone. I just want to focus on You!

Appearances Are Deceiving

"Not so, my lord," Hannah replied, "I am a woman who is deeply troubled. I have not been drinking wine or beer; I was pouring out my soul to the Lord. Do not take your servant for a wicked woman; I have been praying here out of my great anguish and grief."

1 SAMUEL 1:15–16 NIV

When Hannah prayed in the house of the Lord, Eli the priest mistook her for a drunken woman. When he confronted her about the issue, she was quick to correct him with the truth.

First of all, she admitted to being a woman who was deeply troubled. Second, she told Eli she was pouring out her soul to the Lord. Third, she wanted to clarify that she wasn't a wicked or drunk woman. And finally, she reiterated that she was praying out of great anguish and grief.

If you're praying in a public place in great anguish and grief, hopefully you won't need to clarify your motives or explain what you're doing. Just in case you need to, though, boldly admit you're in the middle of a heart-wrenching time and need to pray. Anyone should be able to sympathize with that.

Father God, when I'm troubled, I want to come to You in prayer. I don't care what anyone else thinks about the way I pray—I need You!

The Prayer of the Destitute

For the LORD has built up Zion; He has appeared in
His glory. He has turned His attention to the prayer
of the destitute and has not despised their prayer.

PSALM 102:16–17 NASB

Not many people gravitate toward the destitute. Considered completely impoverished, the destitute usually find themselves forsaken, deserted, neglected, and despised.

Yet the Lord of the universe doesn't forsake the destitute. He doesn't desert them. He doesn't abandon them. In fact, He turns His attention to their prayers without disdain or rejection.

No matter how humbly you perceive yourself, know that the Lord will hear your prayer. Even in moments when you feel low and destitute, know that the Lord of heaven and earth turns His attention to you.

Lord God, thank You for turning Your attention to
all who seek You. It doesn't matter how the world
labels me—You won't despise my prayers.

Giving Instead of Receiving

"In everything I did, I showed you that by this kind of hard work we must help the weak, remembering the words the Lord Jesus himself said: 'It is more blessed to give than to receive.'" When Paul had finished speaking, he knelt down with all of them and prayed.

ACTS 20:35–36 NIV

Once Jesus completely changed him, the apostle Paul spent his life pouring into others. He endured harsh conditions to travel and spread the Gospel. He faced hardships, beatings, and imprisonment. And he worked hard to help the weak.

Paul realized that throughout his ministry he received many more blessings as a giver than as a recipient. He knew it was better to give than receive, and he freely gave away his time, talent, and treasure, as well as the truth of the Gospel. Paul shared this life lesson with his friends from Ephesus as part of his farewell, and then they prayed together.

Have you learned Paul's secret? Are you working hard to help the weak? Are you in the habit of giving?

Father, please give me the opportunity and energy to bless others by giving generously and sacrificially of myself.

So Many Things

I will give thanks to you, Lord, with all my heart; I will tell of all your wonderful deeds. I will be glad and rejoice in you; I will sing the praises of your name, O Most High.

PSALM 9:1–2 NIV

Have you stopped to think of all the wonderful things God has done in your life? He created you just the way you are for a special purpose that He has planned. He knew your sin would separate you from His perfection, so He made a way to bridge the gap. He sent His Son, Jesus, to earth as a rescuer. When you trust in Jesus to be your Rescuer, you won't be separated from the Lord anymore—and that's something wonderful that deserves your thanks and praise!

Aside from giving you a way out of judgment, the Lord blesses you every day with great gifts. Think of the wonderful people He has brought into your life and all the amazing things He does and provides each day. You can be glad for all of it! You can rejoice in Him, thank Him in prayer, and sing praises to His name.

Lord God, You are so very good to me! You've blessed me in amazingly huge ways, like giving me never-ending life through Jesus, and in smaller, everyday ways too. I'm grateful for it all!

Set Free

Out of my distress I called on the LORD;
the LORD answered me and set me free.
PSALM 118:5 ESV

No one enjoys being distressed. No matter how optimistic you might be, it is never enjoyable to suffer or be stuck in the middle of a painful situation. Yet at some point in your life, you'll find yourself in the midst of trials and hardship.

When those moments of anguish come, you may try to muddle through on your own. You might try to numb yourself from feeling the full effects of the situation through some sort of escape, such as social interaction, food, drink, shopping, travel, or media.

Or you can face difficult times head-on with the One who can help. Instead of trying to escape your struggles, turn to the Lord in prayer. Call on Him in the middle of your distress. As you do, He'll answer you. Even more than simply answering you, He'll set you free from your worries. He'll bless you with an undeniable, unexplainable peace. That's true freedom.

Lord, thank You for being there for me when times are easy and when times are terrible. I'm so glad I can call on You in the middle of my distress and You'll set me free from my fears and worries. Thank You for Your peace.

If and When

*"When your people Israel are defeated before the enemy because
they have sinned against you, and if they turn again to you and
acknowledge your name and pray and plead with you in this house,
then hear in heaven and forgive the sin of your people Israel and
bring them again to the land that you gave to their fathers."*

1 KINGS 8:33–34 ESV

Throughout the Old Testament, Israel was stuck in a sin cycle. Even though they worshipped the Lord their God, the Israelites would embrace sin, face judgment and punishment, then repent and be restored. Instead of happening just once, this cycle repeated over and over.

Before you're quick to judge the Israelites, consider your own life. Are you also quick to fall into sin right after you've promised to follow the Lord? And when you experience hard times and the consequences of your sin, do you turn back to the Lord?

Even if you have the best intentions to devote yourself to the Lord, sin is part of this fallen world. And when God grabs your attention through the consequences of sin, it's easy to see where you've strayed and make your way back to Him.

Just as the people of Israel experienced, when you turn again to the Lord, acknowledge Him, and pray and plead with Him, He'll hear in heaven and forgive your sins.

Father, please forgive me! I've followed sin
and wandered away from You. Please restore
me to a right relationship with You.

Sin's Consequences

*"When heaven is shut up and there is no rain because they
have sinned against you, if they pray toward this place and
acknowledge your name and turn from their sin, when you
afflict them, then hear in heaven and forgive the sin of your
servants, your people Israel, when you teach them the good
way in which they should walk, and grant rain upon your land,
which you have given to your people as an inheritance."*

1 KINGS 8:35–36 ESV

When you make sinful choices, consequences follow. As much as you
may hope your sin will never be discovered, it will be. There's always
a repercussion.

For the Israelites, one of the consequences of their sin was a drought.
When they chose to sin against the Lord, He stopped their rain. King
Solomon realized this consequence and presented some specific requests
to the Lord. He asked God to hear the prayers of the Israelites. And
if the Israelites chose to acknowledge the name of the Lord and turn
from their sins, Solomon asked God to hear in heaven, forgive their
sins, teach them the good way to live, and send rain again.

When you find yourself mired in sin, acknowledge the name of
the Lord. Turn from your sin. Ask for forgiveness and follow the good
way He leads you.

> Father God, You are Lord of all! I've sinned against
> You, and I am so sorry. Please forgive me and
> help me change. I want to follow Your lead!

He Knows Your Heart

"When a prayer or plea is made by anyone among your
people Israel—being aware of the afflictions of their own
hearts, and spreading out their hands toward this temple—
then hear from heaven, your dwelling place. Forgive and act;
deal with everyone according to all they do, since you know
their hearts (for you alone know every human heart)."

1 KINGS 8:38–39 NIV

King Solomon knew the Israelites well and spent a lot of time praying about the need for repentance. He knew the Israelites would sin and would need to turn from their sins and receive the forgiveness only God could give.

Solomon also knew the Lord well. He knew the Lord dwells in heaven and hears prayers. He knew the Lord possesses the power to forgive. He knew the Lord alone knows every human heart. And he knew the Lord deals with everyone according to all they do.

Solomon's insight applies to your life as much as the Israelites' lives. The Lord alone knows your heart. He will deal with you according to all you do. If you know Him and are known by Him, He'll deal with you with love, grace, and forgiveness. What does He see in your heart today?

Oh Lord, I want to be found in You alone!
Please forgive me and save me from my sins.

Listen to My Cry

I cry to you, LORD; I say, "You are my refuge, my portion in the land of the living." Listen to my cry, for I am in desperate need; rescue me from those who pursue me, for they are too strong for me.

PSALM 142:5–6 NIV

When you cry, sometimes you want to be left alone in your misery. But other times you might appreciate knowing that someone has heard you and wants to comfort you. Sorrow is inevitable, but being able to share it with someone else can bring comfort.

Even if no other person is around to see your tears, the Lord hears your cries. He knows your needs and can rescue you from any trouble. You can look to Him as your Safe Place. He's your Protection from any person or thing seeking to harm you. He's your Shelter from the unforgiving storms of life. When you feel overpowered, turn to the Lord. He'll listen to your cry and rescue you.

Lord, I need You! I feel so outnumbered, so overpowered, so absolutely in over my head. I need help, and I know that Your help is the only thing that will save me. I trust You. Please help me!

Call upon Him!

"Offer God a sacrifice of thanksgiving and pay your
vows to the Most High; call upon Me on the day of
trouble; I will rescue you, and you will honor Me."

PSALM 50:14–15 NASB

Have you ever considered what a sacrifice of thanksgiving might feel like?

When the psalmist talks about it in Psalm 50, this thanksgiving is given in the middle of the day of trouble. It's not like the psalmist is giving thanks after experiencing blessing after blessing. This kind of thanksgiving is a conscious choice and effort, and it comes at a cost.

A sacrifice of thanksgiving isn't easy or automatic, but it is possible. In your day of trouble, when you're at your lowest, the psalmist calls you to do three things: give the Lord a sacrifice of thankfulness, fulfill any vows you have made to Him, and call upon Him. When you do, He'll rescue you. In response to His faithfulness during your time of trouble, you'll honor Him. Will this be a difficult choice on your part? Yes. But it will honor and glorify your Rescuer.

Lord God, thank You! Thank You for rescuing me when
I desperately need You. Thank You for working in
my life even on my darkest days. I want to thank You
even when I'm scared or discouraged or disappointed.
I praise You because You are Lord of all.

Praying for It to Pass

And going a little farther, he fell on the ground and prayed that, if it were possible, the hour might pass from him.

MARK 14:35 ESV

Even though Jesus knew He would face the cross, He didn't welcome the experience with joyful anticipation. In fact, in the hours before He was betrayed, He prayed fervently that He wouldn't have to endure what was coming. His praying was intense—Mark wrote that He fell to the ground, and Luke said that in His agony, Jesus' sweat became like great drops of blood falling to the ground (Luke 22:44).

God the Father didn't let the hour pass from Christ. He didn't take this particular cup from Him, because He was sent on a mission to save the world. Sometimes, as intensely as you might pray, the Lord doesn't answer your prayers the way you hope. Sometimes He has a much bigger plan that will unfold. Your job is to trust Him and walk through whatever He puts before you.

Father God, I don't always want to carry out
what You've planned for me. I pray I'll faithfully
do it anyway, no matter how I feel.

Whisper a Prayer

O LORD, in distress they sought you; they poured out a whispered prayer when your discipline was upon them.

ISAIAH 26:16 ESV

An old worship song starts with the words, "Whisper a prayer in the morning, Whisper a prayer at noon, Whisper a prayer in the evening, To keep your heart in tune." This is a great reminder that prayer doesn't need to be shouted, it doesn't need to be said out loud, and it doesn't need to be sung. You can think a prayer, or you can whisper it. God hears any prayer and answers.

When you're in distress like the Israelites were, you don't have to come boldly before God's throne with a declaration of prayer. You can pour out a whispered prayer in fear or in exhaustion. Seek the Lord when you're feeling distressed. And when it feels like you're experiencing His discipline, whisper a prayer to Him.

Father, even when it feels like You're disciplining
me, I still can come to You in prayer. And when I'm
in distress, I still can seek You. I'm so glad You can
be found! I'm so thankful I can pray to You!

You Can Pray Anywhere

From inside the fish Jonah prayed to the LORD his God.
JONAH 2:1 NIV

In case you've ever wondered where you should or shouldn't pray, Jonah's life is proof that you can pray to the Lord absolutely anywhere.

The Lord used quite a turn of events to catch Jonah's attention and set him in the right direction. When Jonah's plans to run away were disrupted by a very large fish, he did what he needed to do: he prayed to the Lord his God from inside the fish. He didn't need to get away to a quiet place to pray. He didn't light a candle or bow down in a specific way. He was trapped in the repulsively smelly and sticky inside of a fish!

Jonah described his plight: "Water encompassed me to the point of death. The deep flowed around me, seaweed was wrapped around my head. I descended to the base of the mountains. . . . While I was fainting away, I remembered the LORD, and my prayer came to You" (Jonah 2:5–7 NASB).

Even if you're at the point of fainting away because of life's circumstances, remember the Lord. Bring your prayer to the One who can answer your plea for help!

> Lord, I may not be praying to You from inside a fish,
> but I'm thankful I can pray absolutely anywhere!

A Confession to Make

I acknowledged my sin to You, and I did not hide my guilt; I said, "I will confess my wrongdoings to the LORD"; and You forgave the guilt of my sin.

PSALM 32:5 NASB

Admitting you've sinned isn't always easy. Confession is humbling because you need to both own up to the fact you aren't perfect and admit you've done something wrong. Like a guilty child caught with one hand in the cookie jar, sometimes it might feel like you need to get caught in a sin before you admit what you've done.

King David kept open communication with the Lord and didn't even try to hide his guilt. Instead, he acknowledged his sin in prayer and confessed to God all that he had done wrong. And what was the result? God forgave the guilt of David's sin.

Guilt can be a powerful force that makes you feel trapped, and the only way out is to confess your sins. When the Lord forgives you, the guilt disappears. What do you need to confess today? How can God free you from the burden of your guilt?

Lord, I acknowledge my sin to You! It might
have been intentional or it might have been
unintentional, but I did wrong. Please forgive me.

Praying over Current Events

Then I turned my face to the Lord God, seeking him by prayer and pleas for mercy with fasting and sackcloth and ashes.

DANIEL 9:3 ESV

When Daniel the prophet examined Jeremiah's prophecies about the desolation of Jerusalem, he sought the Lord. Giving his full attention to the Lord, he prayed and pleaded with fasting, sackcloth, and ashes. This was not a trite prayer about the state of his people. He praised the Lord and acknowledged His greatness then confessed Israel's sin. Daniel acknowledged that righteousness belonged to the Lord but open shame belonged to the Israelites. Finally, Daniel asked the Lord to turn His anger and wrath from Jerusalem and the Israelites. Daniel asked for forgiveness.

Much like Daniel, you may find your own country in ruin, living with the harsh consequences of ungodly choices. When you're grieved by current events, call out to the Lord. Recognize His goodness, and then confess the sins of your people. Acknowledge the way righteousness belongs to the Lord yet open shame belongs to sinners. Finally, ask for forgiveness. Ask for the Lord to turn from His anger and turn the hearts of His people toward Him.

Lord God, I need to stand in the gap for my people! Please forgive us for the awful ways we sin against You. Please turn our hearts toward You. Please heal our land.

How Great!

Oh give thanks to the LORD; call upon his name; make known his deeds among the peoples! Sing to him, sing praises to him; tell of all his wondrous works! Glory in his holy name; let the hearts of those who seek the LORD rejoice! Seek the LORD and his strength; seek his presence continually!

PSALM 105:1–4 ESV

Consider the Lord. Now consider all He has done for you. Does His greatness make you want to burst out in song?

As You consider all He is and all He does, thank Him. Tell other people about what He has done for you. In fact, tell about all His works. Glory in His holy name. Bring honor and praise to Him. Free your heart to rejoice in Him. Seek Him alone. Seek His strength and His presence.

As you magnify the Lord in this way, your life will be transformed by your authentic, heartfelt praise. You'll look and seem visibly different in a very good way as you focus your attention and thoughts on the Lord of all.

Oh Lord, You alone are so great and so worthy of my praise. I glory in Your holy name and rejoice even in the thought of knowing You and being known by You. You are so very amazing.

The Good Hand of God

Then the king said to me, "What are you requesting?"
So I prayed to the God of heaven.

NEHEMIAH 2:4 ESV

As the king's cupbearer, Nehemiah went about business as usual serving King Artaxerxes. Deep down, Nehemiah was perplexed and grieved over what was happening in Jerusalem, but he didn't let his personal life interfere with his job. Or so he thought.

Knowing Nehemiah, King Artaxerxes picked up on the fact that Nehemiah was sad—and the king questioned Nehemiah about this sadness. Imagine if the king of Babylon asked you, "Why is your face sad. . . ? This is nothing but sadness of the heart" (Nehemiah 2:2 ESV). Nehemiah was scared. But he also was honest and confessed his concern for Jerusalem.

Instead of condemning Nehemiah for his sorrow, the king listened to Nehemiah, asked questions, and permitted him to return to Jerusalem and rebuild the walls. As Nehemiah summarized it, the good hand of God was on him (2:8).

In your life, you might be placed in situations that blow your mind. Don't hesitate to pray to the God of heaven, and His good hand just might surprise you!

God of heaven, no matter what is happening in my life, I want to come to You in absolutely every situation. I can hardly wait to see the good ways You'll surprise me!

Calling for Help

*I will exalt you, L*ORD*, for you lifted me out of the depths*
*and did not let my enemies gloat over me. L*ORD *my*
God, I called to you for help, and you healed me.

PSALM 30:1–2 NIV

How many times do you try to carry your own burdens? How often do you try to suck it up and muddle through on your own?

When David was close to death, he didn't try to make it on his own. He called to the Lord for help, and God answered in a big way. He lifted David out of the depths so his enemies wouldn't gloat over him. He healed David. And He helped David. In response, David exalted God, but it all started with a prayer for help.

Your enemies, like David's, may pursue you hotly, or you might wrestle with one of the most serious illnesses of your life. Or maybe you'll encounter circumstances unlike any David ever could've dreamed. Whatever low point you're facing, call to the Lord your God for help. He's there for you!

> Lord my God, please help me! You know what
> I'm facing, and You know I can't get through
> it in my own power or strength. I need You.

Inspiring Others

While Ezra was praying and confessing, weeping and throwing himself down before the house of God, a large crowd of Israelites—men, women and children—gathered around him. They too wept bitterly.

EZRA 10:1 NIV

In the Old Testament, Ezra the priest and scribe was appointed to lead the Israelites back to Jerusalem. When they finally returned to the temple, Ezra was appalled when he realized the sinful state of the Israelites. After tearing his clothing, pulling out hair from his head and beard, and weeping, Ezra bowed on his knees and spread out his hands to pray. He confessed the Israelites' sin while owning up to his own personal remorse and humiliation.

Ezra's extreme reaction to sin struck a chord with the Israelites as they watched him weep and pray. Men, women, and children gathered around him and wept as well. Through his own grief and disgust over Israel's sin, Ezra inspired grief and disgust among all the Israelites. Together, they mourned and repented.

Today, you may not realize who is watching as you pray, mourn, or respond to sin. But people are watching. And as you stand for God's truth, you might inspire others to do the same.

Father, like Ezra, I want my heart to be grieved when I see the extent of sin in this world around me. Please help me stand for Your truth. Please forgive me for the ways I've wronged You with my sinful choices.

Be Still

Be still before the LORD and wait patiently for him;
do not fret when people succeed in their ways,
when they carry out their wicked schemes.

PSALM 37:7 NIV

It's easy to consider prayer as communication that requires words. What are you saying to the Lord? What is He saying to you?

But prayers don't always need to be filled with words. Sometimes prayers can include silence.

Psalm 37:7 encourages you to be still before the Lord and wait patiently for Him, and Psalm 46:10 instructs you to be still and know that He is God. These verses are kind reminders to calm down, cease striving, and surrender. Just stop before the Lord and wait patiently for Him.

Will a still, silent wait feel a little awkward in prayer? Maybe. But give your soul a chance to quiet down before the God of heaven. Give Him a chance to settle your spirit and fill you with His peace.

Lord, I'm relieved I don't always have to know what to say,
and I'm grateful I don't have to work to fill the silences.
Please help me grow in the ability to be still before You.
I want to wait patiently for You and know You are God.

I Prayed for This!

"For this child I prayed, and the LORD has
granted me my petition that I made to him."
1 SAMUEL 1:27 ESV

When you've prayed for a specific request over and over for years, you may feel as though the Lord will never give you the desire of your heart. As often as you pray, those unanswered prayers can feel like they're breaking your heart.

But God hears every single prayer you pray. Sometimes He waits much longer than you'd like to give you the exact answer to your prayers. And when He does give you your heart's desire, it can seem like a wonderful surprise—even though you've been praying for it all along!

In the Old Testament, Hannah was tormented by infertility. Finally, after years of praying for a child, she was gifted with a precious firstborn son. She named him Samuel, saying, "Because I have asked for him of the LORD" (1 Samuel 1:20 NASB). For this child she prayed, and the Lord granted her the petition she made to Him.

> Father, You alone know the prayers I continue
> to pray over and over. Please grant me the
> desire of my heart in Your perfect timing.

Waiting with Patience

I waited patiently for the LORD; he inclined to me and heard my cry. He drew me up from the pit of destruction, out of the miry bog, and set my feet upon a rock, making my steps secure.

PSALM 40:1–2 ESV

For the impatient, patience seems like a painful wait. Yet as part of the fruit of a Spirit-led life, patience is a beautiful gift. The Lord Himself is slow to anger. Moreover, as Peter describes in his second letter, "the Lord is not slow to fulfill his promise as some count slowness, but is patient toward you, not wishing that any should perish, but that all should reach repentance" (2 Peter 3:9 ESV).

In Psalm 40, David shares that he waited patiently for the Lord. Even in the midst of trial and trouble, when David felt like he was in a pit of destruction and a miry bog, he still waited patiently for the Lord to act. And act He did. The Lord inclined to David, heard his cry, figuratively drew him up from the murky mess, and made his feet secure on a rock.

You may feel like you've been waiting a long time for the Lord, but keep waiting with patience. He will bend down and hear your cry. He'll pluck you out of the miry quicksand of life and situate you in a safe, sturdy spot.

Father, thank You for hearing me and rescuing
me. No matter what situation I find myself
in today, I know You can intervene.

Praying for Protection

*They all plotted together to come and fight against Jerusalem
and stir up trouble against it. But we prayed to our God
and posted a guard day and night to meet this threat.*

NEHEMIAH 4:8–9 NIV

Threats might be very real in your life. Just because you follow the Lord doesn't mean you'll have a worry-free, problem-free life filled with safety and security. At times, you may feel like you're in grave danger, but you don't have to feel like you're left alone.

When Nehemiah led the Israelites to rebuild the walls in Jerusalem, he faced very real opposition. Smooth-talking, mocking enemies plotted together to distract the Israelites, fight against them, stop their rebuilding efforts, and stir up trouble all along the way. The situation grew so dicey the Israelites needed to work with one hand while holding a weapon in the other.

Yet the Israelites didn't give in to the pressure. Instead of surrendering to their fear, they turned to the Lord in prayer. They continued praying and working until the walls were rebuilt.

Like the Israelites, continue working on what God has called you to do even in the face of danger. Pray about any concerns, and watch the Lord protect and provide. Like the Israelites' foes, when your opponents see what you've been able to achieve, they'll realize the work was accomplished with the help of God.

Father God, please help me! I want to do the work
You've asked, but I'm meeting opposition on every
side. Please help me carry on in Your strength.

The Goodness of His Love

*Answer me, LORD, out of the goodness of your love; in
your great mercy turn to me. Do not hide your face from
your servant; answer me quickly, for I am in trouble.*

PSALM 69:16–17 NIV

Have you ever stopped to consider the fact that God doesn't need to answer you and your prayers? You could pray and praise Him all day, every day, and it would be appropriate because He's Lord of all. Yet He doesn't have to listen to you, He doesn't have to show you mercy, and He certainly isn't required to answer you.

Out of the goodness of His love the Lord does answer you. In His great, great mercy He does turn to you. He doesn't hide His face from you or look the other way. He doesn't try to avoid you because you make Him feel uncomfortable. He isn't fickle—He isn't filled with favor one day then bent on ignoring you the next day. He and His love are steady and constant. You can count on Him and trust Him completely.

Lord God, Your goodness and Your love really are
absolutely amazing. I'm so thankful for the way You listen
to my prayers and answer me in Your great mercy.

Send Your Doubts Packing

If any of you lacks wisdom, you should ask God, who gives generously to all without finding fault, and it will be given to you. But when you ask, you must believe and not doubt, because the one who doubts is like a wave of the sea, blown and tossed by the wind. That person should not expect to receive anything from the Lord. Such a person is double-minded and unstable in all they do.

JAMES 1:5–8 NIV

Reading this passage from James, describing the way God gives generously to all without finding fault, is a great comfort. And how encouraging to know that you can ask God for wisdom and He'll give it! But there's a catch: when you ask the Lord, you need to believe and not doubt. In fact, doubt has no place when it comes to faith.

If doubt does creep into your mind, remember that it will only blow and toss you around, just as if you were a flimsy boat thrown into a wild, wavy sea. If you entertain and embrace doubt, the Lord considers you to be double minded and unstable. You can't expect to receive anything from Him if you relish your doubts.

Ask God for what you need, but when you ask, make sure you do it with full confidence, faith, and belief. Know the Lord can and will answer your request. Stop doubting the power of the living God.

Lord, I want to believe in You! Help my unbelief!
Please empower me to leave my doubts far behind.

Do You Need to Complain?

*Hear me, my God, as I voice my complaint; protect
my life from the threat of the enemy.*

Complaining usually isn't a very admirable trait. Complainers are known
for being ungrateful and unappreciative. Whining and complaining
seem to go hand in hand. In Philippians 2:14, the apostle Paul clearly
taught to do all things without grumbling and complaining.

Yet in Psalm 64, David asked the Lord to hear him as he complained.
What was going on in David's life to merit a complaint?

David faced more turmoil than most people could ever imagine. His
specific complaints had to do with his enemies' threats and the awful
things his foes said about him. David's enemies plotted and schemed
against him and set traps.

David had a lot of valid complaints. He knew he could talk to
the Lord about his concerns and annoyances. He knew if he had any
chance of survival, it came only from the Lord. He knew God alone
had the power to protect his life from the threat of the enemy.

If you're facing an enemy today, talk to the Lord about it. Be honest
about your concerns, and ask Him for help!

Hear me, Lord God, as I tell You about all my concerns.
Please protect me from the threat of my enemies.

Whatever You Ask

"Truly, truly, I say to you, whoever believes in me will also do the works that I do; and greater works than these will he do, because I am going to the Father. Whatever you ask in my name, this I will do, that the Father may be glorified in the Son. If you ask me anything in my name, I will do it."

JOHN 14:12–14 ESV

Every single person on the planet has a life before Christ. It's only after you decide to believe what He said and to put your faith and trust in Him that you can have a life after Christ.

If you do make the choice to believe in Him, amazing things happen. For one, Jesus promised that whatever you ask in His name, He will do. Why would He make a promise like this? So the Father may be glorified, or honored, in the Son.

Instead of looking at His promise in a "name it, claim it" way, whereby you name a specific blessing to claim the blessing, think of what you're asking Christ. Think of how the Father may be glorified in the Son through your request. Then ask in Jesus' name.

Lord Jesus, I believe in You! I want God the Father
to be glorified through what I ask of You.

Thirsting for the Lord

You, God, are my God, earnestly I seek you; I thirst for
you, my whole being longs for you, in a dry and parched
land where there is no water. I have seen you in the
sanctuary and beheld your power and your glory.

PSALM 63:1–2 NIV

When you consider David's descriptions of his time spent in the desert wilderness, you realize he knew firsthand the harsh reality of a dry and parched land where there is no water.

While he likely felt physically parched on more than one occasion, he experienced a real spiritual thirst as well. His soul thirsted for his God. His entire being longed for the God he sought. He had already beheld the Lord's power and glory and longed to do so again.

When you discover you're in the middle of a spiritual desert, earnestly seek the Lord through prayer. When you're in a dry spell, you're parched and thirsting for the spiritual refreshment only He can provide.

God, You are my God. Earnestly I seek You. My
whole being longs for You. I feel so parched.
Please quench my spiritual thirst.

Into His Holy Habitation

Then the priests and the Levites arose and blessed
the people, and their voice was heard, and their
prayer came to his holy habitation in heaven.

2 CHRONICLES 30:27 ESV

When you realize your prayer comes to the Lord's holy habitation in heaven, you may feel completely humbled. You're living your common-place life wherever you may be on earth, yet you've felt compelled to pray for something. That prayer of yours is communicated directly to the Lord. He reigns right now and for all of eternity in heaven. From His holy dwelling place, He hears your prayer.

Considering His majesty and indescribable holiness is enough to make you ponder the words you're praying. Ponder away; then pray. Just as the Lord heard the prayers of the priests, Levites, and Israelites, He hears your voice as well.

Lord God, You are holy, holy, holy. The whole earth
is filled with Your glory. I praise Your name, worship
You alone, and thank You for hearing my prayers.

He Knows

You have taken account of my miseries; put my
tears in Your bottle. Are they not in Your book?

PSALM 56:8 NASB

When you're so disappointed your heart feels broken, you may find
yourself weeping and feeling like no one understands what you're going
through. Surely no one sees your troubles and all the tears you've cried.
Certainly you're facing these sorrows all by yourself.

But you're not alone. The Lord has seen your troubles. He has seen
all the tears you've cried. He has taken account of all your miseries.
And He loves and cares for you so much that He would even put your
tears in a bottle. He has taken note of all your hurts and heartaches,
sadness and strife.

He hasn't just listened to your prayers, observed your grief, and
moved on. God is for you, and He'll act with your best interest in mind.
As Psalm 56 goes on to say, "For You have saved my soul from death,
indeed my feet from stumbling, so that I may walk before God in the
light of the living" (verse 13 NASB). He saves you from your troubles
so you may walk before Him.

Father, thank You for paying attention to me! Even
when I feel alone, You are there. Even when I feel
heartbroken, You care. I'm so grateful for the way You
take care of me with Your abundant love and mercy.

Have You Asked?

"Ask and it will be given to you; seek and you will find; knock and the door will be opened to you. For everyone who asks receives; the one who seeks finds; and to the one who knocks, the door will be opened."

MATTHEW 7:7–8 NIV

Has anyone ever expected you to be a mind reader? Maybe you ended up unintentionally disappointing your friend because, in fact, you couldn't read her mind. Or maybe someone else wanted you to help him find something, yet when you asked him where he'd already looked, he admitted he hadn't started searching yet.

If you don't ask for something, chances are you won't receive it. If you don't go to the effort of seeking, it will be pretty hard to find something that's hidden. And if you don't knock on a closed door, you'll need to wait a long time for someone to come along and open it.

Jesus compared prayer to asking, seeking, and knocking. Even though the Lord knows absolutely everything, you still should ask Him for what you want. Seek out His truth to find it. When you figuratively knock in prayer, He'll open the door to you. Make some sort of effort by praying; then watch the way God answers.

Lord Jesus, thank You for teaching that it's okay
for me to ask You! I want to seek You with my
whole heart. I can hardly wait to find You.

The Lord Alone Is God

He prayed to him, and God was moved by his entreaty and heard his plea and brought him again to Jerusalem into his kingdom. Then Manasseh knew that the LORD was God.

2 CHRONICLES 33:13 ESV

In the Old Testament, Manasseh was an interesting man. Crowned king of Judah at twelve years old, Manasseh did evil in the sight of the Lord, ignored God's dire warnings, then was captured by the Assyrians. But while he was in captivity, Manasseh humbled himself and sought the Lord's mercy. When Manasseh prayed, God heard his pleading, was moved, and brought him back to Jerusalem. Then Manasseh knew that the Lord alone is God.

Manasseh is a great testimony to the Lord's abundant forgiveness. Even though Manasseh had been happy to do evil in the sight of the Lord, once he realized the error of his ways, he humbled himself and threw himself on the Lord's mercy. In response, God forgave him and restored him to his throne.

If you stray from the Lord, it's possible to humble yourself and seek forgiveness. God will listen to your prayers, know your change of heart, and offer forgiveness and grace.

Lord, You are God! I don't deserve Your forgiveness,
but I'm so grateful for it. Thank You for accepting my
repentance. I want to do what's right in Your eyes!

What Is God's Will?

This is the confidence which we have before Him, that, if we ask anything according to His will, He hears us. And if we know that He hears us in whatever we ask, we know that we have the requests which we have asked from Him.

1 JOHN 5:14–15 NASB

One of the biggest questions a believer may have is "What is God's will?" John writes that if we ask anything according to His will, He hears us. And because He hears, we know He'll provide what we've asked. But how can you know you're asking something according to God's will?

As theologian John Piper explains, you can look at the will of God in two ways: "His will of decree always comes to pass whether we believe in it or not. His will of command can be broken, and is every day."*

If God has willed something to happen, it will happen. But you also can see God's will in His law and commands. You can choose either to obey those imperative commands or to disobey them. When you obey, you're following the will of the Lord. And when you choose to disobey, you're not. If you wrestle with wanting to do the will of God, read His Word. Discover what He has said, and choose accordingly.

Lord, I want to do Your will, but sometimes I get confused about what it might be. Please help me discover Your commands in Your Word. I want to base my life around Your truth!

*John Piper, "What Is the Will of God and How Do We Know It?" Desiring God, August 22, 2004, www.desiringgod.org/messages/what-is-the-will-of-god-and-how-do-we-know-it.

Far More

*Now to him who is able to do far more abundantly than
all that we ask or think, according to the power at work
within us, to him be glory in the church and in Christ Jesus
throughout all generations, forever and ever. Amen.*

Ephesians 3:20–21 esv

As you read what the apostle Paul wrote in Ephesians 3, let the truth sink in. God is able to do far more abundantly than all you ask or think. His power is at work in you, and it's through His divine power that He'll be able to do so much more than you can even imagine.

When you confess with your mouth Jesus as Lord and believe in your heart that God raised Him from the dead, you will be saved (Romans 10:9). It's when you're saved that His power will be at work within you. That's when He'll do far more than you imagine.

As God is working in and through you, stay close to Him in prayer. Praise Him for all He has done and will do. Ask for His guidance and help. Confess when you're feeling weak and when you've sinned. Ask Him for forgiveness. Humbly bring all requests to Him in honor and love; then trust Him to work in you and in the world for His glory.

Lord God, I'm amazed that You're willing and able and
ready to do so much more than all I can ask or think.
I'm humbled to realize Your power is at work within
me. Thank You! Please help me! I can't live a victorious
life on my own, but I can do *anything* with You.